So You're Looking for a Pastor?

The Practical Guide for Pastor Search Teams

By Chad Balthrop and Page Cole

Table of Contents

ENDORSEMENTS

"This is a practical and extremely helpful tool for any pastor search committee. The authors have given attention to the most important steps for the successful process of calling a pastor. The appendix is loaded with useful tools. Every search team will find great profit in using this tool as a guide."
Dr. Anthony L. Jordan, Executive Director-Treasurer, Baptist General Convention of Oklahoma, OKC, OK

"When asked to write one paragraph about "So You're Looking for a Pastor?" I thought that's easy as I had written several forwards and endorsements over the years for books. But, then I read the book and realized the "So You're Looking for a Pastor?" is filled with so many priceless insights that it was difficult to narrow down what to write. There are many reasons to utilize "So You're Looking For A Pastor?", but if for no other reason the Sample Pastoral Candidate Survey Questions and the comprehensive list of questions at the end of the book are unbelievable. If your leadership team in search of a pastor uses the principles in this book I believe you will choose the right candidate for your next pastor."
Jay McSwain, President, PLACE Ministries, Alpharetta, GA

"Churches will benefit from this simple yet detailed Pastor Search guide. I greatly appreciate the focus on prayer found throughout!"
Mike Napier, Personal Evangelism Specialist, Baptist General Convention of Oklahoma, OKC, OK

"Every church will face the task of seeking the direction of God in light of the needs of the congregation. Christian leaders deal with their calling in light of God's Kingdom all the time, but how does the local church go about this momentous task? Yes they want God's absolute direction, but how does that reduce to finding the person that will be leading the local church for possibly decades. The following pages are a great guide. The authors speak candidly about the necessities of the God side of the picture… such as focused prayer. However, there is great care given to the individual characteristics of the local expression of God's kingdom and

how a group of God-called people can find God's special person for their shepherd. Churches would do well to read these pages and incorporate their wisdom before starting on their very important journey."
Gerald Wessels, D. Min., Peachtree City, GA

"This is a solid book from two solid pastors."
Joel Engle, Pastor of Preaching & Vision, ChangePoint, Anchorage, AK

"This book will be a wonderful tool in the hands of a pastor search team. It is very practical and full of wisdom. You can read in its pages the "voice of experience" from those who have traveled this road before. The book is "down to earth" and includes topics that are often overlooked. Highly Recommended!"
Dr. Bill Pierce, President, Baptist Village Communities of Oklahoma, OKC, OK

"Our pastor of 27 years announced his retirement. We now face the daunting process of replacing this much-loved, well-known Pastor. I am grateful for this wonderful book that will help us navigate the unknown and extremely critical time in the history of our church."
Aaron Lynn, Associate Pastor, Wedgwood Baptist Church, Ft. Worth, TX

"Chad and Page have completed a tremendous guide for the Pastor Search process. This tool will help the search team, the church and the candidate walk through each step in praying for the will of God and to help the ministry begin and flourish. The entire church can and should embrace the process and contribute in a great way. The tool is Christ centered, concise and will bring the church together."
Bill Shiflett, Worship Pastor, Lenexa Baptist Church, Lenexa, KS

"What a practical resource to help any church in the process of guiding a body of believers through the calling of a Senior Pastor! Every church is unique, yet we all have a common need for clarity when it comes to hiring any staff--especially the Senior Pastor. Chad and Page have written an excellent book to guide you and your congregation through this important journey. From their own experience and the experience of walking with

others through this, they have thought of all the details to be taken care of as you listen to the leadership of the Holy Spirit."
Jim Lehew, Associate Pastor, Emmaus Baptist Church, Moore, OK

""So You're Looking for a Pastor" is a much-needed book! It is encouragement, instruction, and inspiration in one package. And it is extremely well written. I only wish I had this book years ago as a staff member trying to help Pastor Search Committees walk through the often difficult maze of calling a Pastor to lead the church. There is so much practical advice to help churches make the best staff choice for ministry effectiveness. Page and Chad have been through the process of calling a pastor several times over their many years in the ministry. Therefore, the principles you will discover in the pages of this book have been used, tested and proven to be effective."
Dean DeMarra, Worship Pastor, FBC Defuniak Springs, FL

"Page and Chad have done a real service to the church by putting together this piece "So You're looking for a Pastor". It is as insightful as it is practical and will be useful guide to any church that is facing the challenge of seeking their next pastor. My own church is beginning this process right now and I am grateful to have this tool to put in the hands of our search committee."
Bill Stinson, Administration and Education Pastor, FBC Alexander City, AL

FOREWORD

If you have walked through the grueling journey of the pastor search process, you have probably recognized that the experience can be similar to a tense season of "The Bachelor". Like the Bachelor, all those involved will get dressed in their best. Everyone will fix their hair and put on a happy face. As the process goes along, there will be temptations to stretch the truth in their favor just a bit. There will be emotional moments when tears flow and hearts are shared with authentic passion. Both sides will share a blunder or two, while passionately articulating their greatest hopes and grandest dreams. After "dancing together" at late night meetings, the search team will have to wrestle through the top candidates trying to decide who is "number one", as the final pastoral candidates helplessly wait to see which one will be chosen. All the while, the entire congregation anxiously waits to see who will actually receive the rose.

Well, maybe there is no rose at the end of the journey but the Pastor Search Process does have the ominous feel of a Bachelor finale. However, in spite of that fact, the Pastor Search process is both a wonderful and a challenging experience for a church, the Pastor Search team, and the Pastor who is praying about a move.

Even though, the pastor search process takes tremendous effort from all those who are involved, it is important to remember that it is a joyful journey and an honor to be a part of God's supernatural purposes in His church. Since it does accomplish a supernatural purpose, you will soon discover that God will use this book in your hand to help you through every step. In fact, the process laid out in "The Pastor Search Process" is not only grounded in the Word of God, but it is a systematic manual that was forged in the trenches of a church and a pastor searching for God's will for a congregation and a community. This book is an answer to prayer because it became a proven process that not only led to the calling of a pastor but it also moved a group of people to dependence on the Holy Spirit.

I trust that as you walk through this process, you will discover the great joy in the journey of searching for a pastor. I pray that God will move you to the center of His will as you faithfully and effectively serve Him and your church. As the process moves forward, my prayer is that the Holy Spirit will use these steps to guide your team to accomplish His Supernatural purposes by leading to the man called to serve your church and your community.

Sincerely,

Chris Wall, Senior Pastor
First Baptist Church
Owasso, OK

INTRODUCTION

"God is putting all the right people in all the right places to accomplish His purpose in our lives, our families, our church and our community."

This statement is true for every individual in your church. God has led you, your current Pastoral Staff, the members, even visiting guests within your church, into this moment. At no time is this more apparent than when a church seeks a new Pastor.

Churches come in all different denominations, sizes, conventions and flavors. They vary in worship style, doctrinal beliefs and church government. Nothing influences the direction of a church more than the process they use to locate and employ pastoral staff.

This workbook focuses on churches whose form of government and denominational structure allow the individual church to seek out, interview and make the final decision to call and hire pastoral staff.

Because every church is different, every Pastor Search Team will be a unique expression of the heart of the church. Entrusted by their church family, this group must come together to contribute, combine and possibly even overcome their personal histories and hang ups, passions, preferences and personal agendas to determine God's direction for their congregation. As this happens they will move the church to discover the person God is leading to be their pastor.

It may seem overwhelming. Where do we start? What do we do? How can we get this right? This resource is a roadmap for your process. Every church is different, but recognizing and employing these best practices will guide your team as you serve your church to fulfill this significant and holy task.

SECTION 1- CREATING A PASTOR SEARCH TEAM

Church...You Gotta Pray!

Dr. Mike Compton once said, *"Man's major mistake is that he gives primary effort to secondary concerns."* Prayer is the starting point of every successful Pastoral Search Process. This is

true for the team, the church and every candidate involved in the process! Sometimes enthusiasm over beginning a new season of ministry or the pressure that comes with the need to fill a leadership position can distract us from what matters most.

Your goal isn't to fill a position. Your goal is to find God's leader for your congregation. Did you catch that? It's not about finding "A" leader, or a "likeable" leader. It's not as simple as "knowledgeable" or "skilled". All these things are important, but remember the Old Testament. Saul looked like a leader, but David was a man after God's own heart. Nothing is more important than discovering the leader God has prepared for your congregation.

Faithful, focused, deliberate prayer is the primary way to be influenced by God's leadership in this process. This is more than

a prayer to begin or close a meeting. It's unhurried time together, as a team, praying for one another, the church and the people God will involve in this process. Make no mistake. Prayer is the key to success. Make the decision early as a church and as a search team to "Always be joyful. Never stop praying. Be thankful in all circumstances, for this is God's will for you who belong to Christ Jesus."
I Thessalonians 5:16-18

Follow Leadership from the God of Order

The Scriptures and Church Bylaws should be the guiding influence for all your actions and decisions. Scripture tells us,

"For God is not the author of confusion but of peace, as in all the churches of the saints."

That same passage encourages us:

"Let all things be done decently and in order."
1 Corinthians 14:33, 40

God is not the author of confusion. Follow the direction and procedures already laid out in God's Word and by the church. Where there is uncertainty, seek clarification. If members of the team are unsure about something, encourage discussions with current staff or the church body to settle confusion. This is not the time for personal political agendas or pettiness. It's important for everyone to know, understand and act according to the agreed upon process.

Let's pause here to highlight an important idea.
Defining your practice for calling pastoral staff is best decided BEFORE you need it.

While your leaders are in place is the best time to consider and refresh your *process* for calling pastoral staff.

If this process doesn't already exist then the take time to have the necessary conversations that empower your team to clearly and prayerfully define your process for the entire congregation.

Seek Counsel from Current Pastoral Staff

Some churches have multiple pastors that oversee specific areas of ministry. These pastors have been called to lead and have invested their lives and families in your church. It's critical for Search Teams to seek leadership, wisdom and involvement from current pastors on your staff. God, and the people of your church have empowered these pastors for "such a time as this". It is their calling to lead and serve well. Their involvement can amplify the quality of this experience together.

Their level of involvement will vary from church to church, but your team must have a long-term view of their responsibility. The leader they call to be Pastor will begin ministry in your church alongside the existing leaders. Your team can position current and future pastors together for success by respectfully considering the experience and insight of your current pastors. Their  counsel, questions and perspective are invaluable to a church and Search Team as seek God for a pastor.

Once the search process is underway, one member of the Search Team should communicate with one member of the Pastoral Staff on a regular basis. This enables clear communication and is vital to a healthy process. Most likely this will the chairman of the Search Team and the most senior member of the Pastoral Staff.

Don't Rush the Process

Everyone wants the process to move quickly and smoothly. Don't sacrifice speed for sloppiness. Moving rapidly isn't the same as moving rightly. Doing things with excellence and with patience will pay off in the long run.

This principle permeates every part of the process. Your meetings shouldn't be rushed. Allow ample time to review resumes, vet the list and interview potential candidates. This is not an encouragement to be lazy or arbitrarily slow about the work, but rather a challenge to do things rightly and in order, even if that means moving slower and more methodically.

Remember, this happens on God's timetable, not yours. God has not forgotten your church, your situation or you. Be patient, and know that it's during times without a pastor that a church can lean more heavily on God than ever before. Churches have been known to pay off debt, hire new staff and set new records in growth during the absence of a pastor.

Slow & Cautious Are Your Best Choices

If church bylaws & policies don't exist, then move with purpose and caution. Without the leadership of a pastor, groups or individuals within a church can make decisions they might not normally make with a pastor present.

Obviously, now is not the time to revamp Church Bylaws. However, discussing with the church and clearly communicating the decisions about the Pastor Search Team and the process they follow is a critical part of the process. Allow ample time for the church to receive, question, understand and be involved in the process. This will minimize the possibility of conflict now or in the future of the process.

Determine Criteria for Search Team Members

Your church may have already determined guidelines for the qualifications of Pastor Search Team Members. If so, follow them. If not, determine your church's beliefs about the scriptural qualifications of someone serving in a role this significant and influential. Those qualifications might include church membership, spiritual giftedness, and consistency in attendance or faithfulness in giving.

Determine Team Size

A variety of considerations impact the optimum size of a Pastor Search Team. The logistics of traveling to hear potential candidates may cause a church to limit the size of a team. On the other hand, some may want a larger number of people involved in the decision. Others may recognize that individual volunteers are busy and may have to occasionally be absent. Generally, a good team consists of 5 to 7 members, with one alternate member who attends all meetings, and votes only when necessary.

Establish Methods for Nominations & Election

When nominating individuals to serve on a Pastor Search Team, it's best to receive nominations from church members only. Give church members several weeks to submit nominations. Those nominations can be submitted in a variety of ways. Nomination forms can be inserted into church bulletins, passed out in small groups or available in the church office. Those names can then be verified against the pre-determined criteria for Pastor Search Team Membership and then placed on the ballot to be elected by your church.

Your church may decide to have the election for the Pastor Search Team during one formal service time. While this is the most common method of electing a Pastor Search Team, you might also consider a "polling" method, whereby church members can vote over predetermined period of time by signing for and receiving a ballot at a table in your church foyer, or in the church office. This allows more church members to be involved in the election process and includes people who may have a calendar conflict with the voting process.

Over Communicate, Over Communicate, Over Communicate

Churches are made up of people. Generally, people are down on what they're not up on. It's amazing how satisfied people are, even if they don't get their way, when they know their concerns have been heard. People get upset when they feel left out, uninformed or misinformed. Qualification, nomination and election of Pastoral Search Team members should be clearly communicated on a broad basis for several weeks using every communication tool the church regularly uses. Then, and only then, should you take your next steps forward.

My Notes

"Gracious words are a honeycomb, sweet to the soul and healing to the bones" Proverbs 16:24.

Section 2- Meetings That Work

Prayer Must Be the Cornerstone of Your Efforts

Start every meeting with everyone praying. Regardless of the kind of meeting, whether it's the meeting where people are nominated and elected to serve on the Search Team, or the celebration service following the first Sunday of the new pastor on the field, every meeting should begin and end with prayer. Commit to this principle. It will surprise you what God will do in you, through you and maybe even in spite of you.

As a search team, develop a prayer schedule with the church body, including worship times, small groups and special age or focus groups. Give everyone a chance to participate in seeking God's will and direction through this process.

Put together a prayer list for everyone to use. It can include, but shouldn't be limited to the following suggestions:

a) Pray for the people involved (Your future pastor & family, Search Team, all candidates for the position, current pastors, church members, current and guests visiting your church during this interim time).

b) Pray for special needs as your team sees them. For example, pray for unity in the church and Search Team; pray for focus and vision for everyone involved; pray for the finances of your church during this interim time; pray for the continued vision and ministry of church as well.

c) Pray for direction from God. Your team cannot and should not move any faster than the Spirit of God leads them. This is HIS church, HIS process, and ultimately it is HIS person for this leadership role that you are seeking. Ask God to give your team wisdom, discernment and discretion.

d) Pray for spiritual protection. When a flock is without a shepherd the devil likes to attack. Even though you may have other staff, your church is in a spiritually vulnerable position, and you likely see issues of spiritual warfare increase in number and severity. Take those issues to God in prayer, and ask for His intervention and blessings!

What else do YOU think you should pray for?

e) _____

f) _____

g) _____

h) _____

Set Your Meeting Schedule

Unless laid out by policies or church bylaws, it is up to you, as a Search Team, to determine when, where and how you will meet.

Will you meet every week, more than once per week, monthly or bi-monthly?

Your meeting schedule needs to include time limits for each meeting. This helps keep your team focused and on course, and can eliminate the "rabbit chasing" discussions that waste time and produce little.

Various Kinds of Meetings

> *Prayer Meetings* – There may be times when the team or the church needs to come together for no other reason but to pray. These times can be guided by a current staff member or by a printed agenda. They can be with the entire congregation or in small groups. Do any or all of them— you can't pray too much!

> *Planning Meetings* – These meetings serve a variety of purposes. You may need to plan your strategy or brainstorm in preparation for interviews. Don't allow yourself to be distracted during these meetings. Good planning is essential and foundational for everything else the Team will do.

> *Interview Meetings with Church Leaders & Staff* – Before looking at the first resume, it's important that the Team spend time with the Pastoral Staff, church leaders and other groups to gain their input and insight into the

process and ultimate choice for a pastor. Make sure both the Search Team and the groups involved are prepared for the meeting by providing attendees with a list of topics to be covered. Ask participants for their questions beforehand.

➢ *Resume Discussion Meetings* – During these are Team comes together to discuss the applicants and their resumes. It's critical for each member of the Team to come prepared, having already spent time reading and praying over the assigned resumes. It is a waste of the efforts of the rest of the group if a member of the team shows up for these meetings without having done their homework. Every facet of the resume is important and should be part of the discussion. References, tenure in previous positions, even the quality of the document itself – every facet of the resume says something about the applicant.

➢ *Interview Meetings with Candidates* – These may be the most interesting and exciting meetings you have, but they are also the most stressful and spiritually overwhelming. Never forget, this is a spiritual process more than anything else. The enemy will do everything He can to disrupt or interfere with what God is doing in your church and your search for a pastor. Pray, pray hard, pray consistently and when you're finished, pray some more!

Critical Meeting Considerations

Open and Close Well – Meetings need to start and end on time. The person responsible for making this happen is the Chairman of the Team. If any individual regularly has a problem being late it is the responsibility of the Team Chairman to visit privately with them about modifying and correcting that behavior.

Show Up – Meetings need to be a priority for team members. The effective process of the Team is critical to the final result the Team produces. The goal is significant, to call the candidate God has selected for their church. Accepting the responsibility to serve on the Pastor Search Team should be taken seriously, and be treated as one of the most important responsibilities in the spiritual journey for each member of the team.

Know the Plan, Work the Plan – Meetings need a plan, an agenda. The Chairman of the Team is responsible for working with the current Pastoral Staff to establish the agenda for every meeting. The Chairman manages the agenda to insure the Team stays on track during meetings. It is easy for the discussion to get off course or to "chase rabbits". It is the responsibility of the Chairman to keep the group focused and the candidate at ease. Having an agenda in place and in the hand of everyone present helps that happen.

Relax & Refresh – Make sure the environment for your meetings are conducive to a productive meeting. Comfortable seating that includes everyone is important. Make sure that room temperature is pleasant, and that ample refreshments (water, fruit, snacks) are available. If you perceive that your meeting will be longer than one hour schedule bathroom breaks. Be as creative as you look for ways to make this a pleasant, memorable and productive meeting for everyone!

Follow Up – Follow up meetings may be necessary from time to time, especially critical when issues arise or were left unresolved at the conclusion of a previous meeting. If a current member of the Pastoral Staff is not part of the Pastor Search Team the Chairman should plan to meet regularly with one member of the current Pastoral Staff to keep them informed about the progress of the team.

MY NOTES

SECTION 3- BUILDING AN EFFECTIVE PROCESS

Establish Your Process / Path as a Team & Church

Abraham Lincoln once said, "Give me six hours to chop down a tree and I will spend the first four sharpening my axe." Developing and following a plan is essential to an effective process for your Pastor Search Team. This plan becomes the "road map" for the steps you expect your team to move through on its journey. Your process is larger than your Pastor Search Team. At different times you will need information from or need to deliver information to other ministry teams within your church such as, Elders, Current Pastoral Staff, Deacons, Core Ministry Teams, Key Leaders and Small Groups. Preparing and following a road map for the process allows your team to receive and deliver the information each team needs to effectively serve the church.

The following list is by no means comprehensive. It is an excellent starting point for any Search Team to consider. New items can be added, while other tasks might just as easily be removed or reassigned to another team. The order of tasks can be rearranged. You may want other teams or task lists can be brought into the process. Seeking God's will is the number one priority as He uses different individuals, in teams, with their spiritual gifts, talents and experiences to accomplish His purpose for your church.

Many of the activities listed below happen concurrently or in conjunction with activities in other groups. Diversity of activity with unity of purpose is the goal.

Things to consider as you chart a "path" for your Search Team to follow:

1. Church Pastoral Staff / Elders / Deacons
   a. Coordinate to determine vision & direction of church.
   b. Continue to pastor & shepherd the church.
   c. Assess strengths, weaknesses, and opportunities where God is currently working.
   d. Lead efforts to hear God's voice through prayer.

2. Pastor Search Team
   a. Form teams, identify roles, define the process, and communicate the process to the church.
   b. Assess strengths, weaknesses, and opportunities where God is currently working.
   c. Assess the needs of the congregation.
   d. Determine community and demographics needs.

e. Listen to church – meet with staff, conduct survey, talk with individuals and conduct forums for discussion.

f. Seek wise counsel by inviting input from outside sources that can add value to the process.

g. Work with pastoral staff to articulate and define the church vision.

h. Generate a Potential Pastor Profile.

i. Prepare Pastoral Information Package, including information regarding church history, statistics, and organization & area demographics.

j. Find potential candidates from recommendations, submitted resumes and any other means God uses.

k. Screen potential candidates against Pastor profile, through Team discussions and relying on God's direction and influence.

l. Vetting:

    i. Narrow the list to the top 10 candidates using resumes.

    ii. Narrow list to top 5 candidates through submitted videos.

    iii. Narrow list to top 3 through the use of a survey, and invite questions from these candidates. You may choose to do phone interviews with these candidates, and follow up with their references.

iv. Through discussion and prayer, choose the top candidate. Seek unanimous consent from the Team. You may be willing to move forward with less than unanimous consent, but it's best to make that your goal.

m. Invite the top candidate to visit with current pastoral staff.

n. Interview the top candidate & spouse in person. Answer their questions as well.

o. Schedule an on-site visit to their current location.

p. If the Team believes God has clearly spoken, then share that with the candidate, and ask if they agree. If they don't, move on to next candidate. If they do, schedule time for the candidate to come to church to meet with pastoral staff and key leadership for all to discuss this potential move.

q. If all is good, schedule a special weekend to invite the candidate to come in consideration as the new pastor. During this weekend include meeting times for the church in general, current pastoral staff and spouses, Search Team and spouses to meet with the candidate and their family.

r. Present the candidate to the church and seek their approval to call the candidate as pastor.

3. Personnel Team
    a. Prepare salary/benefits package.
    b. Prepare relocation package.
    c. Prepare job description with expectations and responsibilities.
    d. Prepare the structure of pastoral accountability.

Determine Your Guiding Principles as a Team

It might sound simple in your own mind – "We're here to find a pastor. We all know what to do and how to do it!" Nothing could be farther from the truth. Finding a pastor is the destination. The guiding principles for your process are the road you travel and vehicle you use that gets you there. Whether members of your Team have previous experience on a Pastor Search Team or no experience at all, these guiding principles enable you to work together as a team, and educate and involve the church in the process.

Every team member carries a unique history of church life, and life in general. They come together with diverse expectations and experiences that influence how they approach the process. Each brings with them their own set of church, family and emotional baggage. Guiding principles give the Team an agreed upon standard they can use to evaluate the opinions and ideas offered by the Team. This standard makes it easier to identify and set aside personal agendas for the good of the church as a whole. It's critical for everyone involved to understand the ground rules, principles and priorities you share as a team, and for everyone to operate within the same boundaries.

These will vary from church to church, and from team to team within the same church. Your form of church government and current policies will influence many of these guidelines, others  are chosen by the Team or the church. Clarify in writing these principles and practices for your Team. Here are a few examples:

Sample Pastoral Search Team Guiding Principles

➢ The search process will be bathed in prayer.

➢ The search process will be in accordance with church constitution and bylaws.

➢ No candidate will be recommended until the Team is unanimous that the Holy Spirit has spoken and identified God's pastor for our church.

➢ The search process will be as open and transparent to the church as possible.

➢ The search process will actively seek input from the entire church—the Team is strictly acting on the church's behalf at the church's request.

➢ The Team will not put timetables on when God may act.

➢ The Team will protect the confidentiality of all candidates for the sake of the candidate and his current church.

➢ The Team is accountable to the church and will provide regular updates through every form of communication the church currently uses. This could include worship service announcements, the bulletin, email/text/mail, website, ministry team meetings, and in small groups.

➢ The Team will clearly and consistently communicate with the current pastoral staff to keep them informed and involved in the process.

WHAT WOULD YOU ADD?

➢ _____

➢ _____

➢ _____

➢ _____

➢ _____

Secure Resumes

Determine how and where you'll promote your Search. If your denomination has seminaries, associations or denominational conventions you may be able to tap into these resources for resumes.

Your team may discover that a more targeted approach may provide better candidates for your church. Requesting suggestions for candidates from respected sources who already have a basic understanding of the personality of your church will likely produce candidates that fit your current church profile. Talk with local, state or national denominational leaders, even former staff members when seeking resumes.

Determine if advertising with denominational periodicals, ministry magazines or websites are approaches that fit your church needs.

Begin Communication with Various Groups

Elders / Current Pastoral Staff – Every Pastor has strengths and weaknesses, areas where they excel and where they need support. During the Pastor Search Process, consult with existing elders / staff to discover how the strengths and weaknesses of your former Pastor affected the church. Invite them to dream with the Search Team about what characteristics are the most critical for the next pastor to have in order to lead your church into a new season of ministry.

Deacons – Scripture clearly defines Deacons as recognized, respected servants of the church. Regardless of the amount of leadership authority your denomination or church government entrusts to Deacons it is important seek their perspective and wisdom in the search for a new pastor.

Key Leadership – Beyond current Elders and Pastoral Staff or other elected Ministry Team members such as Deacons the church will have key volunteer leadership that has invested significant prayer and skill into the life of the church. These leaders serve as Small Group Leaders, on Ministry Teams or Committees that influence a percentage of the ministry of the church. Invite their input into the process by asking what they look for in a Pastor.

Age Groups – Your church has a demographic. The new pastor will influence every part of that demographic. Meet with leaders, volunteers and participants within those specific subgroups of your church. Students, singles, parents of preschoolers, senior adults, meet with them to discover their hopes for the new pastor. You may be shocked and pleasantly surprised at the input and prayer support your team gains by involving these groups.

Support Staff – The opinion of your secretaries and custodians matters. They are often on the front lines of ministry, answering the phone when someone calls in crisis, responding to requests for resources when ministry events are coming together. The Support Staff has been witness to things no one else sees or hears. They are an invaluable source of insight into what makes a great pastor as well as what the greatest needs of the church may currently be.

Survey Your Teams And Your Church.

Ask everyone what he or she believes God wants in a pastor for your church. See the following survey questions. Take time to edit, delete or create your own questions. Not only will the results from such a survey give valuable insight to your Team about the church, but you will also invite and engage the church members to be a part of the process.

Conduct a simple survey in writing with various groups. It may be beneficial to conduct this survey orally with some small groups. The dynamics of the responses within a group may  give greater insight than individual responses on a survey form.

Asking for input from the church says something powerful to each person. It says, "We trust you. We want you to be involved." The Team may have been elected to lead the process, but the church calls the new pastor. Trust them to be part of the process.

Sample Questions – PASTORAL STAFF

1) What are the parts of our church that you think are really going well with our church?

2) What are the parts of our church that you think really could use some work or adjustments?

3) Concerning our former pastor, what aspects of his leadership & ministry do you think were the best?

4) Concerning our former pastor, what aspects of his leadership & ministry do you think were the least successful?

5) What ways would you suggest that could help us have a great relationship with our new pastor?

6) What ways would you suggest that might help us be a better church for our new and current pastors?

What questions would you add?

7) _____

8) _____

9) _____

Sample Questions - CHURCH
Essentials of Church Priority Focus Questions

1. Prayer Life at the Core
   a. Do we see growth in the corporate and personal prayer life of our members?
   b. Does our schedule, programming and communications validate prayer as a priority?

2. Spiritual renewal & cleansing
   a. Do our people stay current in their confession and heart for personal revival?
   b. Are we consistently challenging people to an intimate walk with God and personal holiness?

3. Preaching/Teaching centered around the Bible
   a. Do our preaching/teaching ministries display a well-rounded approach to communicating a comprehensive approach to all facets of doctrine?
   b. Are we consistently challenging those who preach/teach to a higher standard of preparation and excellence in communication?

4. Passion for Missions & Evangelism
    a. Does our church have a consistent track record in evangelism, discipleship and mission activities?
    b. Are we doing an effective job in challenging new believers to follow up with baptism, church membership and personal discipleship?
    c. What do you see as our strategy for reaching our community for Christ?

5. Dynamic worship
    a. Are our corporate worship experiences successful at leading individuals not only into a momentary but also into a lifestyle of authentic worship?
    b. Do our worship experiences contribute to the unity of our church family?

6. Godly Vision & Strategic Leadership
    a. Does our church have a strong Christ-centered vision and strategic goals for accomplishing that vision?
    b. Are the systems, processes and programs we have in place grounded in seeking God's vision for our ministries and church family?

7. Biblical Fellowship and Effective Church Ministry
    a. Are loving relationships and biblical fellowship benchmarks of church in the community?
    b. Are we consistently working to improve the ministry programs and opportunities we, as a church, use to influence our community and world?

What questions would you add?

1) _____
2) _____
3) _____
4) _____

MY NOTES

SECTION 4- SORTING THROUGH CANDIDATES

Considering Red Flag/White Flag Issues

During the search process you may be inundated with a large number of applicants, with each one believing it was God's will that they be a part of your search process. Your team will need to determine some basic parameters for determining if the applicant is qualified to move to the next level of your search process.

There may be "Red Flags" that could serve as warnings to your Search Team that this particular candidate should be removed from any further consideration. Only your team can determine what those "Red Flags" might be for your church.

This does not minimize the role of prayer in determining God's direction in finding the right candidate. On the contrary, by praying for God's direction in building a list of "Red Flags", you absolutely follow His lead in bringing the right candidate to the forefront.

This list might be the most useful area for current pastoral staff members to assist the PST in developing. Since they have a vocational perspective that the members of the PST don't share, they can offer invaluable input that might not be as obvious to laymen.

Also know that there are things that some churches consider "red flags" that you may discuss, but in truth shouldn't be considered. We call those "White Flags", because they truly should be considered neutral issues.

Sample Pastoral Search Candidate Red Flags

CHURCH HOPPER

Candidates who have moved often (every 2 years or less), or have been at their current church less than a year might cause some concern. They may truly have been following God's calling each time. But it's also possible that they lack the personal skills to develop relationships that stand the test of time, or that they simply bring with them the "bag of tricks" or programs & events that they are comfortable with, and when those have run their course, they are ready to move on to a new location.

REPUTATION

If we discover something negative about their ministry or experience that would cause a red flag. This could be issues of ethics or integrity, a management style that runs roughshod over staff and laity, or other personality or performance issues you might fear would cause dissension in your church or staff, and limit the candidates ability to have a fruitful ministry in your church.

BAD REFERENCES

Negative or lukewarm references, or the unwillingness by an individual to give any kind of reference can be a concern. In talking to staff members they've served with, ask the question, "If you had a chance to serve on church staff with this person again, would you? Why or why not?" Negative answers here may just represent a personality conflict or a negative experience those two individuals had. However it certainly should cause further investigation on your part.

DRINKING BUDDY

Based on your denominational view of alcohol, this could be a huge challenge if alcohol is a part of the candidate's life. The pastor search team is not the place to determine what your church policy is or should be regarding alcohol and its use. Most likely your church already has a practice and belief system on this issue. It would be wise to bring candidates to your church who share those practices and convictions.

MOMMA'S BOY

If he tells us that they sent their resume to make their Mom happy, then that's a red flag for sure! This may sound silly, but it's actually happened! Similar "flags" might include "my friend/pastor/denominational leader told me to send my resume, so I sent it just to keep them happy". If the individual doesn't show a strong feeling that God has pointed him in this direction, then that truly is a red flag.

LACK OF PROFESSIONALISM

If their resume looks unprofessional (errors, poor grammar, etc.) or it's just not done well can be a sign of deeper communication or quality issues. In this age of computers, spellcheck and services that can be hired very inexpensively over the internet to make a resume look professional, a shoddy resume sends a message of laziness and lack of concern over excellence in the details.

GENDER

If your denomination only places men in a pastoral role, then obviously this would raise a problem with any resumes submitted by women. Even if your denomination and local church body approve of both men and women in pastoral roles, your church may feel one or the other is what's best for your church at this time in its existence.

DENOMINATIONAL DIFFERENCES

Although we should fellowship and encourage our brothers and sisters in different denominations, it's best if our pastor is currently serving and is a member of our denomination. This doesn't mean that pastors cannot change their theological or denominational perspectives. But where the senior pastor role is concerned, a team should be cautious before bringing a candidate whose last position was a pastor in a different denomination.

MONEY CRAZY

If a candidate is placing an inordinate amount of questioning or emphasis on compensation, it may be a sign of other problems. The scripture is clear on both fronts. *"The love of money is the root of all kinds of evil"* (I Tim 6:10), as well as *"The elders who direct the affairs of the church well are worthy of double honor, especially those whose work is preaching and teaching. For Scripture says, 'Do not muzzle an ox while it is treading out the grain,'"* (I Tim 5:17-18). Churches are responsible to take care of the financial needs of their pastors. But if a candidate has what your team perceives to be an unhealthy or unbalanced perspective on compensation, be cautious.

STRONG DISCERNMENT

It may be nothing more than an unsettled feeling about the person. It's important that teams be open to these feelings while not allowing them to be the primary governing force. A strong "gut feeling" by one member of your team should not eliminate any candidate, nor should it be ignored. Sometimes God speaks clearly to an entire team, and sometimes He chooses to start that process by speaking through one team member.

White Flag Issues

SINGLE OR NO CHILDREN

Concerns may arise that in the role of senior pastor there needs to be a well-rounded experience of being a husband and a father to adequately pastor. However, a church may miss out on an amazing opportunity if it elects to only consider married candidates. It was the Apostle Paul who, himself a single person, encouraged those who were in ministry and were single (I Cor. 7:8-16)

LACK OF "OUR SIZE" CHURCH EXPERIENCE

If the candidate has never been the Pastor or on staff at a church "our size", this might cause a concern. Upon further review though, nearly all candidates are moving from a smaller to a larger church. Most moves do involve moving to a larger organization with greater responsibilities. Common sense might caution against calling someone who has never managed another staff person into a position managing a large number of staff. But exclusion based simply on the size of their previous churches could cost a committee or a church its best potential candidates.

NO PREVIOUS EXPERIENCE IN THIS POSITION

Be cautious about eliminating any candidate simply because they have "never been a Pastor/ Education Minister/ Student Minister" or whatever! Just because they've never served in that role doesn't mean they aren't the best equipped and the right person for your church in that role. If this rule were followed by every search team, then no new minister could ever serve on a church staff, and no associate level pastor would ever be able to serve as a senior pastor. Your team may have a preference to have someone with experience in the position you are hiring for. But not having that experience is not a legitimate red flag to be concerned over.

AGE

Candidates who are very young or much older might be a concern for some committees. Worries about the inexperience of youth, or possible rigidity, as well as potential challenges with reaching a younger community of much older candidates. However, concerns over age should never be a major concern. God used a young man like David to lead Israel to greatness, and God did amazing things through Abraham & Moses when they were extremely old!

Create a "Potential Pastor Profile"

This profile paints a picture of what you feel would describe

"Moses, we're looking for a game changer.
Show the Egyptian in on your way out."

your top candidates. See the following sample, and use it as a starting point for creating your own "Potential Pastor Profile".

This profile is not intended to be rigid set of guidelines that every candidate must meet to be considered. It should be a flexible guide to assist the team as they seek out a person that best fits the needs of their church for that particular role.

This may include expectations regarding current or expected educational levels, and levels of licensing and/or ordination of the candidate. Your profile may incorporate basic expectations regarding years or kinds of experience, expertise or ministry background.

Beyond that, your team may choose to create a "dream statement" that includes what qualities, spiritual gifts, family or even age frame your team feels would best fit your church. Again, none of these guidelines within a pastoral profile is intended to be rigid or used in a singularly exclusionary manner. This profile simply points a team in a general direction with just a slight bit of focus.

Consider the "Sample Potential Pastor Profile", and then determine if this is something that would benefit your team or not. If so, then come up with your own profile. If not, then don't worry about it and move on with your process!

Sample Potential Pastor Profile

Our Personnel Team has been working on revising the Senior Pastor Job Description, but generally they have set these parameters on Education & Faith History, and the Pastoral Search Team has generally leaned in the direction of these Experience & Age general guidelines...

Education

- College degree
- Master's degree from seminary

Faith History

- Licensed & Ordained by a Southern Baptist church;
- Statement of Faith must be consistent with and not in opposition to the Southern Baptist Convention's 2000 "Baptist Faith and Message"

Experience

- Preferably someone who has served on a staff of a larger Southern Baptist church
- Preferably someone who has managed a group of staff members before

Age

- There are no age guidelines, but given the education & experience expectations, it would most likely be someone at least in their late 20's to early 30's, but no "top end" age. We are not interested in a pastor who wants to coast into retirement, but is ready and passionate about helping our church reach Owasso and continue its growth.

Send Survey Of Questions To Top Pastoral Candidates.

By surveying a short list of candidates your team is able to see their hearts and vision a little more clearly than you might from a resume or application form.

This list of questions does not need to be overwhelming or to specific. This survey should include general questions that give the Search Team a little more personal insight into the personality and perspectives of their top candidates.

Don't forget, your Search Team will have more than one opportunity to ask questions of your top candidates, either over the phone or in person. Keep that in mind as you build your survey.

Your team and staff may have a list of questions that is overwhelming. Determine what questions should be asked on the initial survey, which ones should be saved for an initial or later interview. A good recommendation would be a survey with 25 to 35 questions.

In the following table you'll see a sample of a broad range of questions, their categories, and then their ranking in the following areas:

1) The most important questions overall;

2) The questions that should be included on the survey;

3) The questions that should be asked orally;

4) The questions that should be chunked altogether.

Following the "Question Brainstorm Table", you'll see a sample of a survey that was constructed from those questions. You will also find a much more comprehensive list of potential questions at the end of the book.

Sample Pastoral Candidate Survey Questions

Please provide your answers below each question. If you are unsure or a question seems unclear, please don't hesitate to contact us for clarification.

Type	Question	Rank	Survey	Oral	Chunk
Administration	What new programs have you inaugurated in your present church?	1	1		
Beliefs/doctrine	Do you personally affirm The Baptist Faith and Message?	1	1		
Beliefs/doctrine	Do you have a personal mission statement & can you share it with us?	1	1		
Counseling	Do you consider yourself a counselor? What type of counseling do you perform?	1	1		
Local church	What do you see that you like about our church? What do you see that concerns you?	1	1		
Preaching	Explain your perspective on original sermon preparation versus incorporating other outside material.	1	1		
Beliefs/doctrine	What is the gospel?		1		
Beliefs/doctrine	Is there anything missing from this statement of faith that you would like changed or added?		1		
Church government	What are a senior pastor's primary responsibilities?		1		
Church government	What form of church government and leadership are you committed to? Why?		1		
Counseling	How do you equip church members to provide care to other congregational members?		1		
Family life	How do the pressures of the ministry and expectations of the congregation		1		

Type	Question	Rank	Survey	Oral	Chunk
	impact your family? How have you responded in the past?				
Financial issues	Do you have any outside business or ministry involvements? If so, how involved are you?		1		
Financial issues	Have you ever had financial difficulties? Will you give permission for a credit check?		1		
Financial issues	How would you approach the issues of finance and stewardship with your present congregation?		1		
Financial issues	Do you tithe?		1		
Leadership	What is your style of leadership (hands-on, laid-back, fast-paced, facilitator, CEO?)		1		
Leadership	How would you characterize your understanding of biblical church leadership?		1		
Local church	What is a local church supposed to be biblically? How would you seek to cultivate that identity?		1		
Ministry/programs	What role do you see small groups fulfilling in the church?		1		
Ministry/programs	Describe your philosophy of ministry for equipping the body.		1		
Missions/evangelism	What is your view of missions – world and local?		1		
Missions/evangelism	How would you encourage a congregation to engage in personal evangelism? What tools or program(s) would you implement?		1		
Personal growth	What do you consider your spiritual gift(s) to be?		1		
Personal growth	Describe the role of accountability for a pastor and how that has been a part of your life.		1		
Personal growth	How do you get spiritually refreshed?		1		
Personal growth	What are your favorite books and authors?		1		

Type	Question	Rank	Survey	Oral	Chunk
Personal growth	Do you have plans regarding future education? What role do you believe the church should play in your continuing education?		1		
Preaching	How do you preach (e.g., expositionally, topically, doctrinally)?		1		
Preaching	How do you feel about other staff members preaching at our church?		1		
Staff	What accountability would be expected among staff members?		1		
Staff	How would you respond to other staff members who in your opinion are doing a poor job?		1		
Worship	Describe your philosophy regarding the design, focus & leadership various worship services.		1		
Missions	How involved do you personally expect to be in missions- local, national, & foreign?		1		
Beliefs/doctrine	What are some areas of doctrine that you have seen the church move away from in the last few years that you feel we need to come back to?		1		
Church government	What would be your desired method of church government?	1		1	
Church government	What is the primary role of the deacon body? What responsibilities, priorities or boundaries should the deacon body have in defining our church ministry?	1		1	
Administration	Tell of a recent conflict you had and how you dealt with it.			1	
Beliefs/doctrine	What is your position on the recent movement in churches to become "Seeker Sensitive" or "Seeker Driven"?			1	
Beliefs/doctrine	What are some theological issues that you think are especially important for Christians to get right in this time and place?			1	

Type	Question	Rank	Survey	Oral	Chunk
Beliefs/doctrine	What is you view of the baptism and filling of the Holy Spirit?			1	
Beliefs/doctrine	Do you believe in the doctrines of grace? Why or why not?			1	
Church government	What are your views on the relationship between: the staff, the personnel ministry team and the deacons?			1	
Counseling	Describe your approach to premarital counseling?			1	
Counseling	More recently, sexual misconduct within the church has become a more visible issue. What safe guards have you initiated to protect yourself and the church from such misconduct?			1	
Family life	How do you function as the spiritual leader of your family?			1	
Family life	How do you maintain a quality relationship with your wife?			1	
Leadership	How do you supervise, motivate and develop staff, interns and lay leaders?			1	
Leadership	How do you facilitate change?			1	
Missions/evangelism	Do you personally lead people to Christ? Tell of a recent experience.			1	
Personal growth	Describe your weaknesses and your strengths.			1	
Personal growth	Churches desire a pastor who has personal integrity. What does this mean to you?			1	
Personal growth	How do you respond to criticism?			1	
Personal life	List your hobbies and any other areas of interest apart from ministry.			1	
Personal life	What motivates you as a pastor?			1	
Staff	How do you think staff members should be chosen?			1	
Personal growth	Share what role prayer plays in your daily life and in the life of your church?			1	
Administration	What is the role of the Sunday School?	1			1
Beliefs/doctrine	How do you feel about the use of alcohol?	1			1

Type	Question	Rank	Survey	Oral	Chunk
Beliefs/doctrine	What is your view of abortion?	1			1
Beliefs/doctrine	Is there a confession of faith which better articulates your views?	1			1
Beliefs/doctrine	Describe several ethical principles that guide your work.	1			1
Church government	What is your understanding of the office of deacon?	1			1
Counseling	What role does pastoral care and counseling have in your present position? Give us an example of a typical week of pastoral care activities.	1			1
Counseling	What is your counseling philosophy?	1			1
Family life	How do you balance your life between family and ministry?	1			1
Family life	How involved is your wife in the life of the church?	1			1
Family life	How does your family feel about the possibility of your ministry move?	1			1
Financial issues	Do you have outstanding debts with which you are struggling?	1			1
Leadership	What type of staff environment do you function in most effectively?	1			1
Local church	What do you perceive the major task of the church to be and what do you see as your role in that?	1			1
Local church	What are some of the most important ideas and practices that you think cultivate health in the local church?	1			1
Local church	How do you know a healthy church when you see one? What are the leading indicators in your mind?	1			1
Local church	How do you think churches grow biblically?	1			1
Miscellaneous	Why are you leaving your current position?	1			1
Personal growth	What have you learned in the congregation you now serve that will make you a better pastor?	1			1
Personal growth	How do you cope with stress?	1			1

Type	Question	Rank	Survey	Oral	Chunk
Personal growth	What books have been most influential in your spiritual development? In your pastoral development? Why?	1			1
Personal growth	Describe your day-to-day spiritual life.	1			1
Personal life	Have you ever been charged and/or convicted of a crime?	1			1
Personal life	Who are your pastoral role models?	1			1
Personal ministry	What would you identify as your passion in ministry?	1			1
Personal ministry	What is the most enjoyable part of your current ministry position?	1			1
Personal ministry	In what areas of ministry do you feel most experienced and competent?	1			1
Staff	What experience do you have in leading a pastoral staff team?	1			1
Staff	How comfortable are you in providing direction to staff members?	1			1
Staff	Will you work with our present staff? If after 12 to 18 months it is evident that one or more of your staff members need to relocate, will you give them adequate time (up to a year) to do so?	1			1
Worship	What special services do you like to conduct throughout the year?	1			1
Family life	Have you been previously married?				1
Local church	How familiar are you with the current life of our church? Do you have any questions?				1
Miscellaneous	What attracted you to our position?				1
Miscellaneous	If you could ask us any question, what would it be?				1
Missions/evangelism	What types of outreach programs do you feel are important and relevant?				1
Missions/evangelism	Some people believe a church can become too big. Others feel that every church should become as large as possible. What's your view?				1

Type	Question	Rank	Survey	Oral	Chunk
Pastoral skills	What skills do you bring to this position that you believe will serve you and the church well?				1
Preaching	Are there any topics you feel uncomfortable preaching about, such as finances or current moral issues?				1
Staff	What are your expectations of your staff?				1
Worship	What is your opinion on non-traditional forms of worship (e.g., Theatrical productions, multi-media presentations, etc.)?				1
Worship	How do you view Sunday night worship?				1
Worship	How do you balance worship so it addresses the needs of different age groups?				1
Missions	What do you understand to be the mission of the church?				1
Worship	Are you in favor of a traditional Wednesday night prayer meeting or other types of programs?				1
Counseling	What percentage of your week is normally given to counseling?				1
Personal growth	When given opportunities for time off from your church duties, do you take them and how do you use them?				1
Miscellaneous	Do you have an dress requirements for church attire?				1
Beliefs/doctrine	What is your belief regarding corporate prayer?				1
Personal growth	Are you physically healthy right now? Are you spiritually healthy?				1
Preaching	Do you feel the need to preach every week or do you share the pulpit?				1
Worship	How do your worship styles and music get selected in your church?				1
Beliefs/doctrine	What is your view on women in the church?				1

Type	Question	Rank	Survey	Oral	Chunk
Beliefs/doctrine	What is your view on divorce?				1
Beliefs/doctrine	What is your view on homosexuals?				1
Local church	How important is the preschool ministry to a growing and dynamic church?				1
Worship	Give the time allocation for different activities in an average Sunday				1
Miscellaneous	Social Media/Internet check				
Miscellaneous	Credit check				
Miscellaneous	Health check				
Miscellaneous	Criminal Background check				

"But the LORD said to Samuel, "Do not consider his appearance or his height, for I have rejected him. The LORD does not look at the things people look at. People look at the outward appearance, but the LORD looks at the heart." I Samuel 16:7

Sample Pastoral Candidate Survey

1. What new programs have you inaugurated in your present church?

2. Do you personally affirm The Baptist Faith and Message?

3. Do you have a personal mission statement & can you share it with us?

4. What is the gospel?

5. Is there anything missing from this statement of faith that you would like changed or added?

6. What are a senior pastor's primary responsibilities?

7. What form of church government and leadership are you committed to? Why?

8. Do you consider yourself a counselor? What type of counseling do you perform?

9. How do you equip church members to provide care to other congregational members?

10. How do the pressures of the ministry and expectations of the congregation impact your family? How have you responded in the past?

11. Do you have any outside business or ministry involvements? If so, how involved are you?

12. Have you ever had financial difficulties? Will you give permission for a credit check?

13. How would you approach the issues of finance and stewardship with your present congregation?

14. Do you tithe?

15. What is your style of leadership (hands-on, laid-back, fast-paced, facilitator, CEO?)

16. How would you characterize your understanding of biblical church leadership?

17. What do you see that you like about our church? What do you see that concerns you?

18. What is a local church supposed to be biblically? How would you seek to cultivate that identity?

19. What role do you see small groups fulfilling in the church?

20. Describe your philosophy of ministry for equipping the body.

21. What is your view of missions – world and local?

22. How would you encourage a congregation to engage in personal evangelism? What tools or program(s) would you implement?

23. What do you consider your spiritual gift(s) to be?

24. Describe the role of accountability for a pastor and how that has been a part of your life.

25. How do you get spiritually refreshed?

26. What are your favorite books and authors?

27. Do you have plans regarding future education? What role do you believe the church should play in your continuing education?

28. Explain your perspective on original sermon preparation versus incorporating other outside material.

29. How do you preach (e.g., expository, topically, doctrinally)?

30. How do you feel about other staff members preaching at our church?

31. What accountability would be expected among staff members?

32. How would you respond to other staff members who in your opinion are doing a poor job?

33. Describe your philosophy regarding the design, focus & leadership various worship services.

34. How involved do you personally expect to be in missions-local, national, & foreign?

35. What are some areas of doctrine that you have seen the church move away from in the last few years that you feel we need to come back to?

"Trust in the L<small>ORD</small> with all your heart
and lean not on your own understanding;
in all your ways submit to him,
and he will make your paths straight."
Proverbs 3:5-6

Invite Top Candidates to Ask Questions

This is absolutely critical to the process! You can learn a lot from the answers to your questions, but you can learn even more about a candidate by the questions they ask you.

Your top candidates should be able to ask questions of the Search Team or of your current staff. If your team is hesitant for this to happen, it may signal that there are some critical issues you need to work through together. Transparency shouldn't be something that the Search Team or current staff are afraid to have.

Don't be too introspective, but try to consider both the questions they ask as well as the perceived thoughts or motives behind the questions they ask of your team.

Watch Videos of Top Candidates

In this digital era, nearly every candidate will have videos of themselves preaching or teaching. If they don't have them, then ask them to video themselves preaching. They can deliver that to your team via DVD, or even simpler, upload it to YouTube so that your team members can watch it at their convenience.

Determine Your Protocol

Will you only go on site to listen to one candidate? Will you choose to listen on site to top 3 candidates?

In the past Search Teams might travel to a variety of different candidates' churches to hear them preach and do a brief interview. You may still choose to do so. Remember though, when a search team shows up it can have an impact on the candidates current ministry position.

Determining Appropriate Background Checks

Criminal background check- This should be a standard for any candidate that makes it to your top tier of candidates. It might be unthinkable to you that a pastoral candidate would have a criminal history, or fail to disclose it. You would be wrong. Do not fail to do this basic act of due diligence and protect your church from an avoidable catastrophe later on down the road.

Financial/Credit check- While a pastoral candidate may have a clear criminal background, their financial background may not be as spotless. Everyone makes mistakes, and everyone faces challenges with finances at some point in their life. That being said, you will want to know if there are problems with bad debts, credit issues or bankruptcies in the past of your candidates. This can be very telling about their own money habits and wisdom, and give insight into how they might handle or influence financial decisions of the church in the future.

Physical- While this check is not performed very often, your church may decide to ask its final candidate to have a personal medical physical performed. Churches that have had pastoral staff with significant health problems can be particularly sensitive to this issue.

Social Media- In this digital age, it is amazing what can be discovered about anyone on the internet. Social media sites like Facebook & Twitter, professional networking sites like LinkedIn, or even a quick Google search can provide Search Teams with an abundance of information and insight into potential candidates.

MY NOTES

_____

_____

_____

_____

_____

_____

_____

_____

_____

_____

_____

_____

SECTION 5- AVOID DISCOURAGING YOUR BEST CANDIDATES

Search teams have been enlisted and charged with the noble, intensely spiritual task of following God's heart until they find the pastor He wants for their church. Most individual team members are honored and humbled to be a part of this process. Yet there are things your team or it's individual members could be doing that might distract from the process or discourage the best candidates from considering serving as pastor at your church. Consider the following list as attitudes or activities your team will want to avoid.

Insensitivity

Search Teams who are insensitive to the stress that contact with the pastoral candidate brings with that contact...

Any time a pastor receives a call from a search committee, wave upon wave of emotions, questions and uncertainties are sure to follow. Pastor search teams that are insensitive to the unsettling nature of such contacts are more prone to send out letters in bulk to potential candidates before spending the necessary time in prayer in consideration. It's unfair and borders on cruelty to imply that your church is interested in them as a candidate when in truth you've not even begun to explore that possibility through prayer, research and discussion. Wait until you have a word from God before you send word to candidates. You'll avoid needless discouragement and heartache in many candidates if you do.

Slow Communication

Search Teams that are not conscious of their slow pace or poor communication practices...

Just as discouraging as it can be to respond to candidates too quickly, it can be just as disruptive and discouraging to them if there are huge gaps of time in between communications. If a pastor senses God is moving him and his family, he needs to know that you are going to communicate on a reasonable timetable, even if it is to let him know he is no longer in consideration for the leadership role at your church.

Sneaky or Deceptive

Search Teams that misrepresent the heart, needs or expectations of their church correctly...

Before a pastoral candidate ever meets or visits with your church members, he will spend a significant amount of time with your team members. Churches that have been through challenging times may be tempted to hold back some information or details about the life history of your church family. It may be out embarrassment, or a desire to not be judgmental. But commit to be honest, clear and forthright in your dealings. To fail to do so is unfair and disappointing to any candidate who ultimately uncovers the truth.

Below Average Effort

Search Teams that don't set high standards for themselves in both processes and discovery...

Your church will undoubtedly begin receiving resumes or solicitations of interest regarding your pastoral position. If you don't have a tentative timeline (even if it doesn't have time frames on it), then you should develop one and be willing to share that with candidates. It can help them to not be discouraged by allowing them to understand the flow of the process. Also, be very clear and professional when following up with candidates about what you need from them. If you need a resume and videos of them preaching posted on YouTube, then don't ask them for their "references and some tapes of your sermons."

Weak Prayer Life

Search Teams who fail to spend enough time praying...

Pastors who are feeling led by God to move to another field of service are desperate... desperate to hear from God about where, when and how He wants them to make that next step in their spiritual journey. They need to know that if your search team is talking to him that your team is also talking to God, and talking to Him a LOT. If a pastoral candidate is interviewed over the phone by one team member, or he and his spouse are sitting in your church conference room, it's important they sense that your team has been bathing this process, your church and your future pastor in prayer. If he has been praying intensely for the leading of God's spirit, and your team hasn't been, he will know it and you'll both be disappointed.

Unclear Plan

Search Teams without a clear and intentional plan in place…
Your team needs to let each candidate they contact what the plan for this process is, and how you will be meeting, praying and communicating with him. Certain aspects of this process may already be spelled out in the policies of your church, and others may not. Regardless of what's already been determined or not, your team needs to have a focused plan for the process of researching, communicating with and calling a pastor.

Overcompensating for the Past

Search Teams who overcompensate due to the failures or personalities of former staff members…
Pastoral candidates cannot and should not operate in a vacuum when it comes to the recent history of the church and of former pastoral staff members. But what they do not need is a bashing session of the last pastor, or criticisms of his preaching or pastoral skills. The old adage "If they'll talk bad to you, they'll talk bad about you," is so true. By highlighting the negative experiences of the past you run the risk of jeopardizing your

future. Sarcasm, name calling or character assassinations of former staff have no place in your search process or discussions with pastoral candidates.

Private Agendas

Search Teams who allow private agendas to impact the process...

Unless your church is a brand new church start, then it had "previous pastor" for the role they are searching for now. It's disappointing and even frightening when a pastoral candidate perceives he is being asked questions that seem to have a hidden motive behind them. Playing "guess my mind" with candidates, or the ministry version of "Jeopardy" is childish. Just don't do it.

Frustration with God

Search Teams with closed minds or hearts to surprises from God on the journey...

God truly is a God of Wonder. He told us, "For My thoughts are not your thoughts, nor are your ways." Isaiah 55:8. It is not a matter of "if" God will throw you a curve ball or surprise along your journey to find a pastor, but "when" will it happen! Some search teams seem caught off guard, confused or even upset when things don't go like they had expected. Potential pastoral candidates need to see not only that your team is flexible, but that it's excited to see when God invades their space or the search process with a dose of His creativity. When potential pastors instead see frustration or impatience, it sends a negative message your team doesn't want to send.

Sloppy or Tired

Search Teams who allow weariness to cause them to accept easy paths and sloppiness…

The search for a pastor could last only a couple of months, or it could take a couple of years. Search team members need to understand that they are working on God's timetable, not their own. Sometimes God is spending time to prepare the way- He needs to prepare the church, the staff or the community for the leadership of a new pastor. Other times God may be doing His work in the heart of the pastor who will be moving, or ministering to the heart of the church that will be losing its' pastor. Candidates for your pastoral position will be encouraged if they hear words and see examples of your team patiently waiting on God.

Beyond simply being patient, the evidences of patience or a lack of it can be evidenced in the way your team handles details, performs it due diligence or the effectiveness of its communication with the church. As a pastor is considering that move to your church family, it can be discouraging if your team gives the impression that you're running ahead of God, or have taken the easy or sloppy way through the process.

Dishonest or Afraid

Search Teams who are dishonest or cowardly in communicating with candidates about why they are no longer considering them as a candidate...

This is not to suggest that a search team should be cruel or blunt to the point of meanness. But if there are obvious reasons why your team ended their consideration of a particular candidate, they could benefit from thoughtful, tactful communication of that information back to them. It's not necessarily the job of the search team to "fix" every potential candidate, but God brought them across your path for a purpose, and encouragement is always a good thing.

Unrealistic

Search Teams with an unrealistic view of what they can successfully expect and ultimately have...

When pastor search teams begin their quest, they are hopeful to find a pastor with the preaching talent of Billy Graham, the love of St. Francis, the compassion of Mother Teresa and the wisdom of Solomon. Obviously that's a tall order to fill! Search teams ought not to have unrealistic expectations of finding the best pastor in the world; but they ought to have every expectation of God bringing the very best pastor for their church family to them. It can be disappointing and hurtful to a pastoral candidate if in visiting with them search teams seem to be settling for something less than God's ultimate and best choice for their team and for their church.

Ignore Current Staff

Search Teams who show an unwillingness or lack of effort to involve current pastoral staff in the search process...

Ministry is a team approach. Its teams of pastor and lay people, and of pastors with pastors. For any pastor who is considering coming to your church knows that if he does become your pastor, that he will also be working with a team of other staff. Whether that pastoral staff is one volunteer ministry leader, or a multitude of paid pastors, the level to which they are involved in the pastor search process sends a message loud and strong about the respect level the church has for its pastors.

Poor Follow Up

Search Teams who fail to follow up or communicate in a consistent and fair manner...

Far and above all of the other discouragements, this one registers as one of the most common criticisms of pastoral candidates. Search teams may send an initial contact, by mail, phone or email to let the candidate know his resume has been received, but never hear one more peep from the church or team again. Search teams must follow up with each and every applicant as a matter of respect and professionalism. Pastoral candidates will appreciate this. Many pastoral candidates will not allow more than one church at a time to consider their resume. If you are no longer interested in them, then in all fairness let them know that as soon as possible.

My Notes

SECTION 6- HELP CANDIDATES KNOW YOUR CHURCH

Prepare A Written Profile Of Your Church

This profile should give a well-rounded snapshot of "who" your church is… its mission, ministries, staff, history, etc. Candidates may discover that they don't feel as called to your church as the thought they did!

Describe Key Ministries In Your Church

Include descriptive information about the key ministries within your church. Various programs may have descriptive names that your church and Search Team are familiar with, but an outsider may not.

Provide A Financial Snapshot Of Your Church

This doesn't mean full disclosure of all payroll, giving records and how much money was spent on crackers in the nursery last year. A copy of the church budget, a summary regarding church indebtedness and capital programs,

as well as budgets for affiliated entities (schools, ministry centers, etc.) should suffice.

Summarize Educational, Evangelistic & Worship Ministries

In this summary, you'll want to describe your Sunday School/ Small Groups ministries, when they meet and what is the current attendance average. If your church has a regular evangelism or outreach program, describe it as well. Finally, it would be beneficial for candidates to know what a typical worship service looks like, and what the schedule and time frames for those services are.

If there have been significant changes recently that need to be explained or clarification given, then do so here.

Sample Profile of FBC Owasso Church

Missions

> We're committed to missions locally- We started Mission Owasso, a local ministry that does children's clothing, and reaches out to under resourced families in Owasso, using those opportunities to meet their physical needs as entry points to share Christ; we also regularly do service projects, including VBS at apartment complexes, feeding

people at Thanksgiving, Angel Tree, CR, and local service projects through our men's ministries;

➤ We have a group of men involved with disaster relief with Oklahoma Baptist men, who have assisted in cooking and chainsaw crews following hurricanes, floods & tornados, and one headed to Japan in the fall to assist there with recovery following the tsunami;

➤ Our children's ministry is active in missions. Our 5th graders have gone to other churches to lead their VBS and do evangelism;

➤ Our student ministries are active as well. We currently have about 12 teenagers serving in summer missions around the US & the globe, some through SBC, others through Awe Star Ministries; other student ministry missions efforts have consisted primarily of construction projects, mixed with outreach & evangelism activities for the communities they are visiting; we partnered with a church in Guerrero Mexico for 7 years until the drug cartel ran the pastor out of town;

➤ In the past couple of years we have sent individuals and teams to Cambodia, China, India, Mexico, Arizona & Russia We traveled to some of these countries more than once;

➤ We participate in some mission activities sponsored by Tulsa Metro Association as well.

Giving

➤ Our annual budget is currently around $2.6 million per year;

➤ 5 years ago our building indebtedness was around 4.8 million dollars; currently it is approximately $700,000;

➤ Our church gives to the Cooperative Program as well as to Tulsa Metro association; Currently 2% of our undesignated giving goes into a fund for us to do our local missions projects, 5 % goes to CP, and 1% to Tulsa Metro Baptist Association;

➤ Our church takes up a joint Missions offering at Christmas for Edna McMillan, Annie Armstrong & Lottie Moon offerings.

Attendance

➤ Our Sunday attendance is a little down for the summer, but we're averaging for the year between 900 to 1000 in Sunday School;

➤ Our Sunday morning worship attendance is between 750 to 800 people. We do have Sunday School and worship going on at the same time, both at 9 AM and 10:30 AM;

➤ Our attendance is down in both of these areas from 4 years ago, when the Sunday School attendance average was 1,200 & Worship Attendance was 1,000. However, they are up from where we were 6 months ago.

➤ Our Sunday evening schedule has varied over the past few years; at times there was one service, and at other times we've used that time frame for various discipleship efforts for our church family, especially our adults.

Evangelism

➤ Our church currently uses the FAITH Evangelism strategy to train our people to share the Gospel. We enlist teams of three, one leader and two trainees, to work together for a semester. We've held this outreach training and visitation at various times, either on Sunday, Monday or Wednesday evenings;

➤ We've baptized between 50 & 125 people per year over the last 10 years.

Worship

➤ Style- Our services are a blend of contemporary & traditional, approximately 70% contemporary & 30% traditional. We use a choir, praise team, instrumental ensemble (8 to 15 pieces) for the music. We also make effective use of drama, video, calls to prayer & lighting to enhance worship;

➤ We do use high-def television cameras, and have a fully functioning production booth. We have been but are not currently on television;

➤ Preaching- Our people have shared that they enjoy a variety of styles of preaching- expository, topical, relational and teaching. The sermon time is typically 25 to 40 minutes of the worship service time.

Gather Community Profile Information for Candidates

It's likely that this information has already been assembled, possibly from your Chamber of Commerce or Economic development organizations in your community.

The church operates within its community, and it is important that your candidates understand the mission field they are considering moving into. Most communities will already have available a synopsis or report describing your community for potential businesses or individuals to consider before moving to their community.

Respond To All Candidates Who Send You Their Resume

Many times candidates are unaware of how to or "who to" address their resume. To avoid any confusion regarding whether or not their resume has been received, it's best to simply respond by letter to each candidate who submits a resume.

This same letter can be sent to potential candidates who have their name verbally submitted to the Search Team. The letter can be altered to inform them that their name has been submitted, and let them know that if they wish to be considered as a candidate for the position that they will need to submit a formal resume.

Sample Response Letter

Date

Name
Address
State

Dear ,

The Pastor Search Team of First Baptist Church Owasso has received your information and inquiry of a possible candidate for pastor.

We are in the initial stages of our task. Our congregation has joined in a time of prayer to pray for our search to be directed by the Lord. We are confident of His direction and timing.

At this point, we simply desire to acknowledge we have received your name. If God has led you in a different direction please drop us a note to remove your name from our search.

We pray God directs you in all you do in service to Him.

Sincerely,
FBCO Pastor Search Committee

Contact Applicants No Longer In Consideration

If you reject an applicant, it's fair to contact them and let them know they are not in consideration any longer. Some applicants are only willing to deal with one church at a time, and as long as they think your church is still considering them as a candidate, they may turn down other viable opportunities that are a better fit for their spiritual gifts and experience than your church. In fairness to them, release them if you are no longer considering them.

A simple letter informing them that they are no longer in consideration should suffice. There is no need for specific explanations or reasons they were eliminated. Simply let them know you appreciate their interest, and thank them for their prayers as you both continue on your journey.

Preparing Questions for Pastoral Candidate Interviews

Build a comprehensive list of questions for your interview with any pastoral candidates you meet with. You've already begun this process when you created a survey. Build upon that process by determining the next level of questions that need to be asked in the first and succeeding interviews.

Break down the oral interviews into an initial interview, an interview with the Pastoral candidate and spouse, and questions reserved for the final candidate who will be brought to your campus. There is no right or wrong question in any of these sessions. Your team needs to determine which are best suited for each of these interviews.

My Notes

SECTION 7- KEEPING EVERYONE "IN THE LOOP"

Reporting to the Entire Church

Monthly reports by your Chairman to the church body once per month on Sunday morning is a great way to keep the church engaged and excited about the process. This is even more critical if the process takes a significant period of time. Although every church situation is unique, a good rule of thumb for how long the process should take is 1 to 2 months for each year the previous pastor served as pastor. As you can tell, as the months without a pastor pass, the church body can become anxious or uneasy. Monthly reports help to ease those tensions.

Reports through church bulletins, newsletters, emails and church website are great ways to keep the church informed. The more you communicate with the entire church, the better the process for the PST and for the future pastor.

Informing Your Small Groups

Another great way to keep the church members involved is to send individual members of the PST to Sunday School/Small Group classes to allow people to ask questions on a regular basis.

This allows for interaction between the team and the church. Make sure and provide Search Team members with bullet points of information, so that everyone is reporting the same thing. It's critical that the church sees unity and harmony on the Search Team.

Discretion is crucial when you begin narrowing your list of names. No names of candidates should be shared in these small group times, as it could negatively impact the ministry of the candidates in question.

Meet With Key Leadership Groups Separately

As was suggested earlier, there is much to be gained by gathering input from the Deacons/Elders, Personnel Team, Pastoral Staff, Support Staff, Church Leadership, Sunday School/Small Group Teachers & church members at large. The same can be said for keeping them involved in the process by seeking out opportunities to engage them all throughout the process.

This can be accomplished by having period question and answer periods, and by encouraging PST team members to continue the dialogues with church members outside of those formal meetings. Remember that privacy is critical as you narrow the search, so make sure the PST honors that principle and that church members are aware of it so they don't feel like things are being kept from them unfairly.

Take Care That You Don't Run Off Your Very Best Candidates

Search Teams who are insensitive to the stress that contact with the pastoral candidate brings with it.

Any time a pastor receives a call from a search committee, wave upon wave of emotions, questions and uncertainties are sure to follow. Pastor search teams that are insensitive to the unsettling nature of such contacts are more prone to send out letters in bulk to potential candidates before spending the necessary time in prayer in consideration. It's unfair and borders on cruelty to imply that your church is interested in them as a candidate when in truth you've not even begun to explore that possibility through prayer, research and discussion. Wait until you have a word from God before you send word to candidates. You'll avoid needless discouragement and heartache in many candidates if you do.

Search Teams that are not conscious of their slow pace or poor communication practices.

Just as discouraging as it can be to respond to candidates too quickly, it can be just as disruptive and discouraging to them if there are huge gaps of time in between communications. If a pastor senses God is moving him and his family, he needs to know that you are going to communicate on a reasonable timetable, even if it is to let him know he is no longer in consideration for the leadership role at your church.

Search Teams that misrepresent the heart, needs or expectations of their church correctly.

Before a pastoral candidate ever meets or visits with your church members, he will spend a significant amount of time with your team members. Churches that have been through challenging times may be tempted to hold back some information or details about the life history of your church family. It may be out embarrassment, or a desire to not be judgmental. But refuse to be honest, clear and forthright in your dealings. To fail to do so is unfair and disappointing to any candidate who ultimately uncovers the truth.

Search Teams that don't set high standards for themselves in both processes and discovery.

Your church will undoubtedly begin receiving resumes or solicitations of interest regarding your pastoral position. If you don't have a tentative timeline (even if it doesn't have time frames on it), then you should develop one and be willing to share that with candidates. It can help them to not be discouraged by allowing them to understand the flow of the process. Also, be very clear and professional when following up with candidates about what you need from them. If you need a resume and videos of them preaching posted on YouTube, then don't ask them for their "references and some tapes of your sermons."

Search Teams who fail to spend enough time praying.

Pastors who are feeling led by God to move to another field of service are desperate... desperate to hear from God about where, when and how He wants them to make that next step in their spiritual journey. They need to know that if your search team is talking to him that your team is also talking to God, and talking to Him a LOT. If a pastoral candidate is interviewed over the phone by one team member, or he and his spouse are sitting in your church conference room, it's important they sense that your team has been bathing this process, your church and your future pastor in prayer. If he has been praying intensely for the leading of God's spirit, and your team hasn't been, he will know it and you'll both be disappointed.

Search Teams without a clear and intentional plan in place.

Your team needs to let each candidate they contact what the plan for this process is, and how you will be meeting, praying and communicating with him. Certain aspects of this process may already be spelled out in the policies of your church, and others may not. Regardless of what's already been determined or not, your team needs to have a focused plan for the process of researching, communicating with and calling a pastor.

Search Teams who overcompensate due to the failures or personalities of former staff members.

Pastoral candidates cannot and should not operate in a vacuum when it comes to the recent history of the church and of former pastoral staff members. But what they do not need is a bashing session of the last pastor, or criticisms of his preaching or pastoral skills. The old adage "If they'll talk bad to you, they'll talk bad about you," is so true. My highlighting the negative experiences of the past you run the risk of jeopardizing your future. Sarcasm, name calling or character assassinations of former staff have no place in your search process or discussions with pastoral candidates.

Search Teams who allow private agendas to impact the process.

Unless your church is a brand new church start, then it had "previous pastor" for the role they are searching for now. It's disappointing and even frightening when a pastoral candidate perceives he is being asked questions that seem to have a hidden motive behind them. Playing "guess my mind" with candidates, or the ministry version of "Jeopardy" is childish. Just don't do it.

Search Teams with closed minds or hearts to surprises from God on the journey.

God truly is a God of Wonder. He told us,

"For My thoughts are not your thoughts, nor are your ways." Isaiah 55:8. It is not a matter of "if" God will throw you a curve ball or surprise along your journey to find a pastor, but "when" will it happen! Some search teams seem caught off guard, confused or even upset when things don't go like they had expected. Potential pastoral candidates need to see not only that your team is flexible, but that it's excited to see when God invades their space or the search process with a dose of His creativity. When potential pastors instead see frustration or impatience, it sends a negative message your team doesn't want to send.

Search Teams who allow weariness to cause them to accept easy paths and sloppiness.

The search for a pastor could last only a couple of months, or it could take a couple of years. Search team members need to understand that they are working on God's timetable, not their own. Sometimes God is spending time to prepare the way- He needs to prepare the church, the staff or the community for the leadership of a new pastor. Other times God may be doing His work in the heart of the pastor who will be moving, or ministering to the heart of the church that will be losing its' pastor. Candidates for your pastoral position will be encouraged if they hear words and see examples of your team patiently waiting on God.

Beyond simply being patient, the evidences of patience or a lack of it can be evidenced in the way your team handles details, performs it due diligence or the effectiveness of its communication with the church. As a pastor is considering that move to your church family, it can be discouraging if your team gives the impression that you're running ahead of God, or have taken the easy or sloppy way through the process.

Search Teams who place a higher priority on comfort than clear communication.

It's a reasonable possibility that some of the candidates your team is considering may know each other. It is critical that your team is honest with candidates why they are being removed from consideration, and that your team is honest in communicating those truths. Integrity demands it, and beyond that it's a biblical principal that "your sins will find you out." Candidates in the running may pass on information, or disgruntled members of your team or church might also share facts a team may have tried to keep from coming to light.

Search Teams with an unrealistic view of what they can successfully expect and ultimately have.

When pastor search teams begin their quest, they are hopeful to find a pastor with the preaching talent of Billy Graham, the love of St. Francis, the compassion of Mother Teresa and the wisdom of Solomon. Obviously that's a tall order to fill! Search teams ought not to have unrealistic expectations of finding the best pastor in the world; but they ought to have every expectation of God bringing the very best pastor for their church family to them. It can be disappointing and hurtful to a pastoral candidate if in visiting with them search teams seem to be settling for something less than God's ultimate and best choice for their team and for their church.

Search Teams who show an unwillingness or lack of effort to involve current pastoral staff in the search process.

Ministry is a team approach. Its teams of pastor and lay people, and of pastors with pastors. For any pastor who is considering coming to your church knows that if he does become your pastor, that he will also be working with a team of other staff. Whether that pastoral staff is one volunteer ministry leader, or a multitude of paid pastors, the level to which they are involved in the pastor search process sends a message loud and strong about the respect level the church has for its pastors.

Search Teams who leave candidates hanging for long periods of time, or by not communicating effectively.

Pastoral candidates shouldn't have to assume anything. That would include information about future communications, clear requests for information, and any other needs that the Search team might have. Some teams are quick in their enthusiasm to initially touch base with pastoral candidates to make them aware that they are in consideration for the open position, and then fail to follow up in a timely manner, if ever! Remember that following any communication by a Search Team to a potential candidate, that the spouse and family of the candidate are dramatically affected by this information. Staying clear and fresh in communication is essential for an effective Search Team.

SECTION 8- THE LAST STEP

When You've Found the Right Candidate

The resumes are all put away. You've finished interviews. No more listening to sermons from different candidates or travelling to hear them preach. Your search team has settled on its final candidate, completed your interviews, and it's time to bring him to your church!

It's a feeling of exhilaration, of accomplishment and spiritual satisfaction to be involved in the process of partnering with God to bring His person to your church. But wait! Your work is not over! There still remains the critical task of bringing your pastor to the church for their consideration and approval. There are a myriad of moving parts, special events and a mound of details to make this a satisfying and productive process for both your candidate and for your church. Here are some major considerations for your team to work through as they bring this journey to an exciting celebratory end.

Bringing It All Together

Since every church is different and every circumstance is unique, you'll need to customize the suggestions and ideas in this section to meet the needs and expectations of your church, staff and denomination. Regardless of the many factors that make churches unique, there are several general steps that nearly every church should consider as it calls a new pastor to their congregation.

Among those factors are:

- ➢ Intentional Schedule
- ➢ Privacy Issues
- ➢ Clear Communication
- ➢ Small Group Interaction
- ➢ Practical Considerations
- ➢ Mechanics of the Call

Making the Most of Everyone's Time

As we've emphasized from the beginning of this process, you must plan to pray if you want to stay close to God's heart and His will in this process. Your pastoral candidate and family members are under a tremendous amount of stress at this point. You and your church are simply calling a pastor. He and his family are:

1. Leaving their current church family & ministries behind;
2. Facing the stress of packing and moving to a new home;
3. Helping transition their children to a new school;
4. Leaving behind friendships that are deep and long;
5. Considering the challenges of leading an entirely new set of volunteers and staff and building those relationships;
6. Possibly looking for a new job for the pastoral candidate's spouse;
7. Dealing with the pressure of changing finances during the transitional period;
8. Facing the task of finding new doctors, dependable mechanics, best grocery store, and a myriad of other things you each take for granted.

Now let's think about the people in your church. Is it possible that they need you to lead the way in prayer because:

1. Some may still be dealing with emotional issues over the leaving of your last pastor;
2. Others may have agendas they are waiting to unload on your new pastoral staff member;
3. Staff may be excited, afraid, uncertain or worried about the new pastor…

Now do you understand why it's so critical that prayer be at the top of your list? Pray, Pray, PRAY as a group and as individuals during this most critical time of the journey!

It's also critical that you plan times for your candidate and smaller groups to get together during this part of the process. We'll go into more detail later, but suffice it to say that it's important that you NOT only schedule large group events, but rather give both the candidate and smaller groups the opportunity to interact.

Don't forget to schedule in breaks for the candidate. The stress and pressure are very real, and to give your candidate and his family the opportunity to put their best selves forward, intentionally schedule some "break times" between some of the small group interactions. This will give them a chance to relax, interact privately with their own family, and ask any questions they might have of your team or staff.

In preparation for this series of meetings, go to great lengths to post the agenda for the weekend so that everyone is aware of what is happening, and when/where it is taking place. Even if you are not publishing the name of the candidate yet, you can still promote the weekend events and schedule several weeks in advance.

Everyone Knows When They Need to Know

By this time, you're very excited to let everyone know who the candidate is and where he is coming from. You can't wait to tell them about his family, his ministry and his wonderful gifts! It's at this point your team needs to exercise caution and self-control. At this juncture in a long journey, the last thing you want to do is unnecessarily complicate anything for your candidate or for your church.

Your team understands the need for respect for his current church and situation. As much as local churches want their pastor to follow God's will, it's painful to see when God's will takes them away from your congregation. While many would be understanding, there might be members of his current congregation that would be hurt or confused, and make this portion of his journey more difficult. They will learn soon enough about what is to come.

Not only are you protecting your pastor in his current church situation, but you're also providing cover for him and his family from "enthusiastic" church members. Believe it or not, there are those that would be very comfortable going around your search team, current staff and the process in motion to communicate with the pastoral candidate before they arrive. Whether it's to air grievances, lay groundwork to deal with a personal agenda, or simply to "make friends", these individuals can stress your pastoral candidate and confuse the process if you're not careful to protect the identity of your candidate until the appropriate time.

So when IS the right time to share the names of your pastoral candidate and family members, and their current ministry location? Most churches have found that the Sunday immediately before they come to your church for consideration is the best time to share those specifics. In this technology age, if you share this information any sooner than that, it's not a matter of "if it will get back to his church"; it will get back to them, and that could cause problems or stress that neither your pastoral candidate not his current church need or deserve.

Shout It Loud, Clear & Often

Just because you're being honorable by protecting the identity of your candidate until the week before they come to meet your church does not mean you can't promote this event sooner than that. You should begin communicating about this exciting weekend several weeks before it happens. This allows your church members plenty of time to plan to be involved.

Include an agenda for the weekend in your promotions of this big weekend. Your church members need to know which events are happening, and if they invited to be a part of that particular gathering. A simple calendar of events listing the time, location and people groups invited to that meeting should suffice.

One fun and unique way to introduce your pastoral candidate to the people of your church is to invite the members of your church to write a card to the pastoral candidate and/or each of his family members. You can publish this information the Sunday before they come to your church. It's a great way to build excitement and energy for the event. If your pastoral candidate has children or teenagers it can be very helpful to them if the children and teenagers from your church write notes directly to those students, welcoming them to their church for the coming weekend!

There are a variety of ways to get the word out to your church about the big weekend. Use the church website, mail things out to church members using the church mailing list, put out a special edition of your church newsletter, include special inserts in your weekly church bulletins and use social media like Facebook, Twitter or Instagram to promote the events that make up this special week in the life of your church family.

Small Groups Make for Intimate Introductions

Regardless of the size of your church, it's beneficial to your church members and the pastoral candidate and his family if you have some small group times built into this weekend. Here are a few suggestions for you to consider.

Schedule a welcome dinner on Friday night with the members of your Search Team, your current pastoral staff and their spouses. Cater in the dinners so everyone can focus on enjoying the experience and not worrying about the details of the meal. Be sure that your location is large enough to comfortably accommodate everyone having a meal. The agenda for this time can be very general. Eat, laugh, celebrate and enjoy building relationships around a fellowship meal. That's more than enough to make this a perfect event.

Other examples of small group meetings might include those groups of key leadership- Deacons, Elders & Personnel Team are just a few examples of those types of groups. These leaders will work alongside your pastor to chart and implement the strategies and activities for leading your church to follow and do God's will. Everyone is a disciple, but these are key leaders, and as such need they may have unique questions or encouragement for their incoming pastor. These meetings don't have to be long and drawn out, but they are very important. Don't forget to ask for input from your incoming pastoral candidate when planning for these meetings.

Another critical meeting would be with the leaders of your church Small Groups. The best church growth happens when people are involved in a small group that disciples, encourages, stretches and matures its members. Great pastors know these truths are real, and should be given the chance to meet with these leaders to establish their partnership in the discipleship process.

If the pastoral candidate is leading in a specialized or age level ministry, consider the value of having a special time with the candidate and the people within that ministry. If he's a Student Pastor, then schedule a time for your students to have exclusive access with him to both meet him and ask questions. It's important that the people within these special areas of ministry feel included in the process.

Whatever small group meetings you choose to schedule, it's important that you have an agenda for each meeting that includes a time for candidate to give a brief introduction of himself and family, and his heart for ministry, as well as a question and answer time.

Food, Facilities and Free Wifi

When your pastoral candidate shows up for this special weekend of meetings and consideration, he needs to have no worries when it comes to the basic necessities of the weekend. The best rule of thumb here is "Assume NOTHING, communicate EVERYTHING!"

More often than not, your pastoral candidate does not currently live in your community. If this is the case, then someone on your church staff or search team needs to make hotel reservations for your candidate and his family. Don't be a cheapskate. Get them a quality room at a nice hotel in a good location. If there is a large family, spring for two adjoining rooms rather than one room with uncomfortable couch beds or roll away beds. Typically you will be making reservations for Friday and Saturday nights, but if there is no rush for them to return to their current home, then include Sunday night as well.

Transportation costs should not be something that is left unclear or uncertain with your candidate. If your candidate will be traveling by car, then calculate their round trip mileage, plus expected travel while they are your city, and then multiply that total mileage by the current mileage reimbursement rate allowed by the IRS. If your individual will be flying to your community, you'll want to reimburse those flight costs as close as possible to the time they make their reservations. Having a representative meet them at the airport is very important, but your church should also provide a rental car so that they are not "trapped" in their hotel room at times where they are not at the church for meetings or services.

Meals are another vital consideration. Plan your schedule for the weekend, and then consider providing a very gracious "Pre-imbursement" for the candidate to cover their meals during those times where the church will not be directly feeding them. This includes covering those meal times during their travel to and from your church from their current home.

For a special touch, consider creating "Welcome Baskets" for each member of the family. Have these in their hotel room waiting for them when they arrive. They could include fruit, snacks, bottled water or other small gifts. Be sure to include a note from either your staff or your search team, and let your candidate and his family know how excited you are that God has brought you all to this point!

Voting to Call Your Pastor

Although some denominations assign pastors to serve with their congregations, we're assuming that isn't the case with your team, since you're reading his book! Evidently your local church plays some part in the calling and relocation of pastoral staff. Since that's the case, consider these important facets of the process of successfully navigating the "calling" process:

Your church most likely has either a Church Constitution, a set of Church Bylaws or a combination of both. Within documents like these, many of the issues addressed below may already be addressed. If so, then follow those directions. If not, or if they are unclear or general, then work with your current staff and leadership to clarify the following issues:

Your search team will need to determine the place & time of voting to call your pastoral staff member. Will this take place during a worship service? At the end of a worship service? Using ballots and a polling place following the service? Your team needs to bring clarity here, and share those details in all of your communications about this weekend.

Your team may need to make clarifications and communicate WHO actually votes as you call a pastor. Some churches require that only church members vote, or that individuals be a church member AND of a certain age to vote. Other churches are much more flexible in their membership and allow attendees to vote. Whatever your situation, make sure that the requirements and expectations for voting are spelled out clearly before the event, and most certainly when the voting is actually taking place.

If your church bylaws do not dictate how the votes will be cast or counted, then again it is critical that your team work with your current church staff and leadership to determine and communicate with the church what the method of voting and counting those votes will be. Many churches require a certain percentage of affirmative votes in calling a staff member. If yours is one of those churches, be aware of that percentage, and make sure that those counting ballots are aware as well. One final consideration in voting is whether or not your church has, does or will require individuals to sign their ballot as they vote. Regardless of what your church or leadership decides is the standard in this decision, it's very important that you communicate that standard to people effectively.

Finally, determine where your pastoral candidate and his family will be during the voting process, and who will be with them. This is a very stressful time for them, and it is much better for them if they are in a room separate from where the voting is taking place, rather than left to sit on the front row of the church while their future is being decided! Once those results are known, the pastoral candidate and his family should be told those results in private first. It is critical that your team will need to work with the current staff and leadership to determine the timing and method of announcement of those voting results. But only after the results are shared with the pastoral candidate should the results shared with the church as a whole.

SECTION 9- THE CRITICAL FIRST YEAR

Be Available to Your Pastor & His Family

Any move can be difficult on a family. Changing jobs is just as stressful. Add to that the pressures of leaving old friends and familiar places behind, financial pressures and changing work relationships and you have the ingredients for a perfect storm of uncertainty and tension.

The members of your team can relieve some of this tension by being available to your pastor and his family members. They have known your team the longest, and are likely to be most comfortable with you and your team members. Encourage the members of your team to initiate contact with him and his family on a regular basis. It doesn't have to be a formal meeting or scheduled event. But it does need to happen, and it will if your team members plan to do it intentionally.

Ask questions about how the transition and move are going. Inquire about their living arrangements, about the neighborhood and schools. Be concerned that they are finding their way around a new town ok, and ask if they are having any trouble finding the "important" people in their new surroundings- people like mechanics and pediatricians, hair stylists and appliance repairmen.

Go the extra mile and offer encouragement in a variety of ways. Send a note to the kids with a gift card enclosed to a local hamburger joint. Ladies, grab the pastor's wife and steal her away for a quick Starbucks break. Invite the pastor to go for a Saturday game of golf, or an evening at the gym. While you have their attention, find ways to work your own, sincere words of encouragement into the conversation. Remind them regularly how thankful you are that God brought their family to your church. Trust that God will bring just the right encouragement into their lives at just the right time... and be crazy enough to believe He might use you to be the one to bring it to them.

Plan 6 Month Celebration with Pastor & Team

The first six months your new pastor is at your church can be a whirlwind experience, both for him and his family. Sometimes things are so crazy and filled with so much change at once that they may miss some of the fantastic things happening around them and through them. Help them to focus on the great things happening in your church. Point out the growth in the church ministries, the positive changes in people's attitudes and the differences you see happening because of the impact and service of your pastor and his family.

But do more than just point out what's going on. Give your pastor and his family chances to talk about their dreams for the future. Invite them to open up about what they want to see God do in their own lives, in your church and community. Ask to brag on God for a minute about what they have seen Him do in the past six months, and what their long term dreams are for their own spiritual walk, as well as what they pray the impact of the church will be on your community and world.

Finally, this is a good juncture to see if there are any practical things he or his team need. Are they finally unpacked, and are there any home needs they might have? What about his office-any equipment or staffing needs that are critical and yet going unmet? Find out how you can help, and what you can do to make their next six months even better than the first.

When the First Year is in the Rearview Mirror

Anniversaries are great times to reflect, give thanks and take in all that God has been doing. Why not schedule a pizza party following your Sunday evening service, and invite the church to come and celebrate with you! Before the meeting, challenge the search team members to list out the victories and landmarks of this past year. Invite your church members to do this as well, and as you enjoy some pizza and good fellowship, give people a chance to share their own testimonies of victory and vision about what God has been doing!

Before this event, invite the church to write out notes of affirmation and encouragement to the pastor and family, and present them as a gift during this time of fellowship. If you plan well, you can assign one or more people in the church to document with pictures and video all of the exciting things happening in your church throughout the first year. Then in the month prior this celebration event, enlist someone with technology skills to put together a celebration video!

A special bond is formed between the members of a Pastor Search Team and the pastor and his family during the search process, their call to your church and their first year of service. Make the most of that time, those relationships and the opportunities God provides along the way to continue to bless your pastor and his family.

SECTION 10- APPENDIX

Appendix A- Sample Church Survey

ABOUT YOU

Gender: ◉ Male ◉ Female

Age:
◉ Under 20 ◉ 20—29 ◉ 30—39
◉ 40—49 ◉ 50—59 ◉ 60+

Marital Status:

◉ Never married ◉ Married ◉ Separated/divorced ◉ Widowed

Children at Home: Do you have children under 18 living at home?

◉ YES ◉ NO

Level of Participation: Describe your level of participation.

- ◉ Not very active (once a month or less)
- ◉ Somewhat active (@ least twice a month)
- ◉ Active (@ least three times a month)
- ◉ Consistently Active (@ least once per week)
- ◉ Very Active (more than once per week)

Walk with Christ: How would you describe your walk with Christ?

- ◉ EXPLORING—I believe in God, but I'm not sure about Jesus. My faith is not a significant part of my life.
- ◉ GROWING—I believe in Jesus and I am working on what it means to get to know Him. I'm learning about the Bible.
- ◉ CLOSE to CHRIST—I am really close to Christ and depend on Him for daily guidance. I have a solid understanding of the Bible.
- ◉ CHRIST CENTERED—My relationship with Jesus is the most important relationship in my life. It guides everything I do. I know the Bible and apply it to my life.

ABOUT OUR CHURCH

Purpose: What is the purpose of (your church name)?

Ministry Involvement: In which ministry are you most active?

- Senior Adult
- Adult
    - Christian Arts Ministry
    - Sunday School
    - Discipleship University & FAITH
    - Celebrate Recovery
    - Mission Projects
    - Missions
- Students
    - Children
    - Preschool

Which current area of ministry at our church do you feel is the strongest?

Which current area of ministry at our church do you feel needs attention?

Is there an area of ministry you feel our church should be involved in that we are not?

Evaluate the following areas of our church. How well do these ministries challenge, equip and encourage you in your journey of faith?

	NONE	SOME	OKAY	A LOT	VERY MUCH
SUNDAY SCHOOL	1	2	3	4	5
DISCIPLE UNIVERSITY	1	2	3	4	5
WORSHIP SERVICES	1	2	3	4	5

In our Worship Services, I prefer the MUSIC to be:

- More Traditional (older hymns/praise songs/fewer instruments)
- More Contemporary (newer songs, upbeat arrangements, modern instrumentation)
- Best of the Old with the Best of the New (a variety of songs, both old and new, done in a variety of ways, using a variety of instruments)

In our Worship Services, I prefer the PREACHING to be:

- EXPOSITORY, verse-by-verse—allowing Scripture to speak for itself.
- TOPICAL—focus on relevant topics from a Biblical perspective.
- RELATIONAL—stories of faith that illustrate Biblical truth and challenge and inspire people to action.
- I LIKE IT ALL—as long as it's based on the Bible!

How well do these ministries challenge, equip and encourage your child in their journey of faith?

	NONE	SOME	OKAY	A LOT	VERY MUCH
PRESCHOOL | SUNDAY	1	2	3	4	5
PRESCHOOL | WEDNESDAY	1	2	3	4	5
CHILDREN | SUNDAY	1	2	3	4	5
CHILDREN | WEDNESDAY	1	2	3	4	5
STUDENT | SUNDAY	1	2	3	4	5
STUDENT | WEDNESDAY	1	2	3	4	5

Do you serve as a VOLUNTEER at our church?

⊚ YES

⊚ NO

Do you serve as a VOLUNTEER in a responsibility at our church you believe you are called by God to fulfill?

⊚ YES

⊚ NO

ABOUT OUR SENIOR PASTOR

Priorities: Of the ministry priorities of our church, which THREE does the incoming Pastor need to emphasize the most? (CHECK THREE ONLY)

WORSHIP

- Preaching & Teaching
- Leadership vision & compelling plan for the future of our church
- Prayer

DISCIPLESHIP

- Developing small Bible study groups/classes
- Organizing & empowering volunteers for ministry

FELLOWSHIP

- Building relationships in which people are connected & care for one another

MINISTRY

- Care for the poor (social compassion)
- Strengthening families

EVANGELISM

- Sharing the gospel in our community
- Missions Involvement—leading our church to serve the church of God around the world through giving, going and sharing the gospel

Strengths: Which TWO of the following do you consider the most important strengths needed in a Senior Pastor? (CHECK ONLY TWO)

- Preaching / Teaching—An effective communicator

- Vision Casting—charting the course for the future of our church & implementing the plan to achieve that vision.

- Administration—skilled at handling the business of the church.

- Pastoral Care—Counseling individuals, making hospital or prospective member visits

- Personal Preparation—through prayer, Bible study, preaching preparation.

- Personal Involvement—in individual ministries, fellowships & 'church life'.

First Baptist Owasso Fact Sheet

First Baptist Owasso is your place for faith, family & friends. We are a purpose driven Southern Baptist Church and support both the Baptist Faith and Message and the Cooperative Program of the Southern Baptist Convention.

We believe that Jesus Christ is the hope of the world and the church is His plan for sharing that hope with the world.

Our mission is to lead people to become fully devoted followers of Christ. We accomplish this purpose through a variety of ministries designed to equip and encourage Believers to share the gospel and invest their lives in the lives of others. Across the street or around the world you will find members of First Baptist Owasso sharing the love of Jesus.

Fully Devoted Follower

At First Baptist Owasso we are leading people to become fully devoted followers of Christ. Every ministry of the church is wrapped around this one idea. Within these ministries you will discover opportunities to build lasting friendships as you learn from God's Word and experience Him in worship. There are opportunities to learn, serve, lead and grow. Some are for everyone. Some are just for you.

What Does It Mean to Be A Fully Devoted Follower?

Being a fully devoted follower of Christ doesn't mean you're perfect. But a fully devoted follower is easy to identify. You can think of it like this, "A fully devoted follower of Christ studies God's Word and prays daily, is involved with other Believers; and actively seeks to make God-honoring choices in their life."

Let's unpack that a little further.

Healthy Appetite + Healthy Activity + Healthy Choices = Fully Devoted Follower of Christ

Healthy Appetite

For a fully devoted follower of Christ a healthy appetite means you have a hunger for God's Word and prayer. There is within you a constant desire for spiritual things and the classic spiritual disciplines of the faith. Someone with a healthy appetite will learn to feed themselves through personal Bible Study and devotionals. Prayer won't be the emergency phone call in times of crisis, but will be a pattern for everyday life. A healthy appetite for spiritual things doesn't mean you'll be perfect. But it does mean you will, on your own, be growing closer to God each day.

Healthy Activity

For a fully devoted follower of Christ healthy activity is church involvement. There are literally hundreds of ways you can be involved at First Baptist Owasso. Every growing Believer should connect with the church in at least three unique ways:

Small group Bible study – this is Sunday School, a place to build lasting friendships as you study the Word of God together.

Worship Services – Every Sunday the people of First Owasso come together for worship. Dynamic music, and video combine with the relevant, life changing messages from the Word of God to bring all the people of First Owasso together in worship.

Individual Connection – Whether you need help with parenting or finances, whether you like to sing or serve with children, we believe everyone should have some kind of individual connection with the church. For some people this will mean deepening their walk through a Disciple University Class. For others it means volunteering or leading within one of our ministries. Whatever your stage of spiritual development you will find a place for an individual connection at First Baptist.

Healthy Choices

For a fully devoted follower of Christ healthy choices are choices that reflect obedience to God's Word. The things you do to feed your healthy appetite, the opportunities you take for healthy activity, these will help you make healthy choices as you grow in Christ. None of us are perfect, but as we grow in Christ we should eventually learn to avoid those things that trip us up and pursue those things that bring glory to God — that's what making healthy choices is all about.

For more information about First Baptist Owasso visit http://www.fbcowasso.org. Watch services online @ http://www.lifeponits.tv.

First Baptist Owasso Fact Sheet
CHURCH MEMBERSHIP: 2,786
SUNDAY SCHOOL ENROLLMENT: 3,342

Preschool:	322
Children:	1,089
Students:	513
Adults:	1,418

AVERAGE ATTENDANCE

2010	*Worship:*	777
	Sunday School:	956
2011	*Worship:*	733
	Sunday School:	889

NUMBER OF BAPTISMS
40
55 (to date)

BUDGET
$2,563,496
$2,400,000 (proposed)

MISSIONS GIVING: 8%
Cooperative Program: 5%
FBCO Direct Missions: 2%
Tulsa Metro Baptist Network: 1%

CAMPUS DEVELOPMENT
The people of FBCO owe $520,000 on the current campus. We reduce this mortgage by a minimum of $37,100 per month. $35,000 of this comes from the Annual Operating Budget with designated giving providing the rest or allowing us to give more than the $37,100 monthly minimum.

While a Master Plan was completed several years ago there are no current plans for future construction. The prevailing spirit is that we should become debt free as soon as possible and, as God provides, future construction should be accomplished without debt.

LEADERSHIP STRUCTURE

The people of First Baptist Owasso believe that Jesus is the head of the church in all things. Under the direction of the Holy Spirit, First Baptist Owasso is Pastor-led, Deacon-served, Team-managed, and Congregationally approved.

The Deacons function within their Scriptural mandate to *serve* the church. They are not a governing body. Rather, they provide insight and accountability for the Ministerial Staff.

The Pastors and Ministry Staff provide leadership in all matters of spiritual direction, teaching, ministry programming, strategy and priorities.

The Pastors and Ministry Staff lead alongside Volunteer Leaders and through Volunteer Ministry Teams. Three of these Ministry Teams go through a process of election and selection by the Congregation, Pastors and Ministry Staff and Deacon Servants of the Church. These three teams are the DEACONS, PERSONNEL TEAM and FINANCE TEAM.

All other Ministry Teams are overseen directly by the Pastor or Ministry Staff member directly responsible for that area of ministry and are formed on an 'as needed' basis. Members of these teams are selected and approved by the Pastors and Ministry Staff.

We currently have a total of 16 Ministry Teams with numerous sub-teams.

Current Team Listing:
Elected & Selected
Deacons
Personnel Team
Finance Team

Age-Level
Preschool Ministry Team
Children's Ministry Team
Student Ministry Team
Senior Adult Ministry Team
Adult Ministry Teams:
Sunday School
Disciple University
Women's Ministry
Men's Ministry
Celebrate Recovery

Missions
Mission Owasso
Missions Ministry Team

Worship Services
Christian Arts Ministry Team
First Impressions & Greeters Ministry Team

CITY OF OWASSO

Director of Economic Development

Chelsea Levo

918.376.1518 direct

918.346.2665 cell

clevo@cityofowasso.com

www.cityofowasso.com

Economic Profile

The City Without Limits.

Household Income

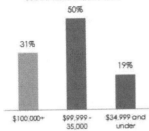

- 31% — $100,000+
- 50% — $99,999 - 35,000
- 19% — $34,999 and under

$21.25 million
Annual Retail Sales

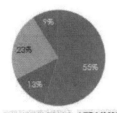

- 9%
- 23%
- 55%
- 13%

EDUCATIONAL ATTAINMENT

- ■ High School Graduate
- ■ Associate Degree
- ■ Bachelor's Degree
- ■ Master's Degree or Higher

PRIMARY TRADE ANNUAL LEAKAGE	$933,636,330
Non-Store Retailers	$322,069,393
Furniture & Home Furnishings	$23,283,792
Appliance, TV, Electronics Stores	$23,790,229
Build Material & Supply Dealers	$35,817,663
Other Build Materials	$41,468,121
Special Food	$37,053,275
Pharmacies & Drug Stores	$57,782,284
Women's Clothing	$12,024,031
Shoe Stores	$7,876,464
Jewelry, Luggage, Leather Goods	$46,013,312
Sporting Goods	$37,411,728
Sewing, Needlework & Piece Goods	$5,033,309
Book, Periodical & Music	$6,631,838
Gift, Novelty, Souvenir	$5,993,145
Full-Service Restaurants	$68,572,371
Limited Service Eating Places	$50,264,849
Special Foodservices	$15,201,097
Drinking Places	$9,984,168
GAFO Clothing & Clothing Accessories	$60,037,903
GAFO Furniture & Home Furnishings	$23,283,792
GAFO Sporting Goods, Hobby, Book, Music	$44,043,566

MEDIAN HOUSEHOLD INCOME	$71,849

FAMILY HOUSEHOLDS 78%

TAXES	
City Sales and Use Tax	3.5%
County Sales Tax, Tulsa	0.917%
County Sales Tax, Rogers	1.833%
State Sales Tax	4.5%
Total Sales Tax, Tulsa Co.	8.917%
Total Sales Tax, Rogers Co.	9.833%

	Estimated 2015 Population	Annual Growth 2000 - 15	Estimated Annual Growth 2015-2020
CITY LIMITS	33,539	4.31%	1.89%
ZIP CODE	42,484	3.67%	1.76%
FENCELINE	50,003	3.99%	1.80%
PRIMARY TRADE	244,447	1.27%	0.35%

Community Profile

The City Without Limits.

AGE

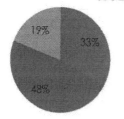

- 19%
- 33%
- 48%

■ 20 and Under
■ 21-54
■ 55 and Over

COST OF LIVING

$72,116

Median Household Income

$191,000

Median Home Price

$865

Median Rent for a Two-Bedroom Apartment

ETHNICITY

- 12%
- 3%
- 7%
- 78%

■ White
■ Black
■ Hispanic
■ Other

TRANSPORTATION

20 minutes

Median Travel Time to Work

Closest Airport

10 minutes

TEMPERATURE

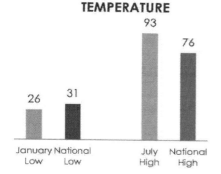

- 26 — January Low
- 31 — National Low
- 93 — July High
- 76 — National High

Expansion Management determines the Quality of Life for a community by evaluating nine criteria. Owasso excels in all nine areas of evaluation.

1. Access to Air Travel

Owasso is located 10 minutes from Tulsa International Airport which serves 3 million passengers annually

2. Lack of Traffic Congestion

Owasso Public Works continues to upgrade and improve our streets to prevent traffic congestion and to provide ease of access to our growing residential and retail properties all over the city. Owasso has fewer accidents per capita than the national average.

3. Quality of Workforce

Owasso's young, educated residents make exceptional employees, and with one million potential employees within a 30 minute drive of Owasso, your business will have an exceptional workforce from which to choose.

4. Standard of Living

Quality youth sports programs and several well maintained community parks offer families recreational and leisure activities. Owasso's crime rate is well below the national average, despite the growing population. This level of safety and security cannot be found in larger cities. One of the many benefits of locating in Owasso is small town living with big city amenities just 15 minutes away in Tulsa.

5. Quality of Schools

Owasso Public Schools are among the highest ranked in Oklahoma and are ranked above average nationally. The student population has grown to over 9,800 students. The Owasso School District provides excellent physical facilities and equipment to support a quality program that meets the educational needs of the students. There are also private and faith based educational opportunities available.

6. Adult Education Levels

With just over a third of the population possessing some type of college degree, Owasso ranks ahead of the Tulsa area and the state in education attainment.

7. Continuing Education

Owasso has 12 colleges within a 45 minute drive, and a Tulsa Tech campus with a Tulsa Community College partnership opened in Owasso in fall of 2013. Partnerships with Oklahoma State University, the University of Oklahoma and the University of Tulsa as well as top technical and vocational training facilities ensure a highly trained and efficient workforce for your company.

8. Housing Affordability

Housing in Owasso is not only affordable, but diverse. Owasso is a leader in the region in housing starts. Owasso is also growing in renting and leasing options between housing, apartments, duplex or mixed use development.

9. Peace of Mind

Owasso's crime rate is well below the national average, despite the growing population. Services including police, fire and EMS are provided by highly trained, well-equipped, and strategically located personnel to assure a quick, effective response to any emergency.

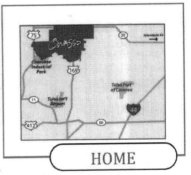

HOME

The City of Owasso is proud of its heritage, encouraged by its present growth, and excited about its promising future. The City & Chamber will continue to work hard to make Owasso an increasingly attractive place for businesses and families to call it their home.

Appendix D- Sample Candidate Questions Listing

Spiritual Journey Questions ✓

a) Ask the candidate to share his full testimony of salvation.

b) Have him identify key people God has used in his spiritual journey.

c) After his salvation experience, did he ever struggle with doubts and if so how did he overcome his doubts? What are his primary spiritual gifts?

d) Ask how he defines his primary gift or gifts. Let him give examples of ways God has most used his spiritual gifts to impact Christ's kingdom.

e) What are some situations when he felt somewhat inadequate or uncomfortable?

f) Have him describe his most challenging personal and ministry difficulty.

WHAT QUESTIONS WOULD YOU ADD???

g) _____

_____

h) _____

_____

i) _____

_____

Personal Life Questions

a) Ask the candidate to share about his family and upbringing (i.e. his father and mother, siblings, their work, church involvement, where they lived, etc.)

b) What were some of his greatest joys and memories?

c) Ask about hobbies and things he enjoys on his day off or vacation.

d) Have him describe his various work experiences (both church and secular).

WHAT QUESTIONS WOULD YOU ADD???

e) _____

_____

f) _____

_____

g) _____

_____

h) _____

_____

Family Questions

a) Let the candidate tell how he met his wife.

b) Have him share about their wedding and early years together.

c) Ask him to describe his family devotions. How often do his family devotions take place?

d) Let him share his wife's special interest, talents and hobbies.

e) Have him tell about his children and how each one is unique.

f) Ask him to describe some of the unique family challenges of being "in the ministry."

g) How has his family responded to some of the challenges of being in the ministry?

h) How could a church help minimize pressures on his family?

WHAT QUESTIONS WOULD YOU ADD???

i) _____

_____

j) _____

_____

k) _____

_____

l) _____

_____

Ministry Questions

a) Ask the candidate to describe his call to the ministry.

b) Have there been times of doubting his call and if so, how did he work through such times?

c) Ask him to describe the different types of ministries he has performed.

d) What ministries did he like most and least?

e) Is he happy and fulfilled where he is presently serving? Why or why not?

f) Why does he believe God may be calling him to another position? (This question is absolutely crucial!)

WHAT QUESTIONS WOULD YOU ADD???

g) _____

_____

h) _____

_____

i) _____

_____

j) _____

_____

Education Questions

a) Let the candidate share how college and seminary helped prepare him for the ministry.

b) If he has a doctorate, ask its topic and how it has impacted his ministry.

c) Does he have plans to pursue any more academic degrees?

d) Ask him to identify some of his spiritual heroes. Why did these people have such great impact on his life?

e) What is his overall philosophy of effective pastoral ministry and leadership?

WHAT QUESTIONS WOULD YOU ADD???

f) _____

_____

g) _____

_____

h) _____

_____

i) _____

_____

Philosophical Questions

a) How does he define an effective, healthy church?

b) Ask the candidate to describe particular times in his life that caused him the most spiritual growth.

c) What specific lessons did he learn from his special times of challenge?

d) Ask him to share his greatest dreams for his life, ministry and family.

WHAT QUESTIONS WOULD YOU ADD???

e) _____

_____

f) _____

_____

g) _____

_____

h) _____

_____

Revival Questions

a) Ask the prospect to describe his understanding of the difference between an evangelistic meeting and genuine revival.

b) Has his church experienced what he would call genuine biblical revival? Why or why not?

c) Has he led any of his churches to conduct solemn assemblies or something similar?

d) How important (or practical) does he think such emphases are in today's Church?

e) Does he believe most churches need periodic times for church-wide cleansing, relational healing and renewal? Why or why not?

WHAT QUESTIONS WOULD YOU ADD???

f) _____

_____

g) _____

_____

h) _____

_____

i) _____

_____

Unity Questions

a) Determine if the prospect has a strong record of leading his churches and staff to unity and peace.

b) Determine in detail the various controversies or divisive issues he has encountered and how he handled them.

c) Ask if there are any particular pressures that make him want to leave.

d) What are his strategies for strengthening church fellowship and creating a positive spirit of joyful togetherness?

e) Ask about his strategies for preventing and minimizing church controversy and division.

WHAT QUESTIONS WOULD YOU ADD???

f) _____

_____

g) _____

_____

h) _____

_____

i) _____

_____

Vision Questions

a) Determine his long-term, personal and ministry goals?

b) Have the candidate describe his understanding of helping a church find their God-given vision.

c) Ask the prospect if his church has adopted short and long term strategic visions or plans.

d) Does his church embrace a yearly vision or strategic goals? Why or why not?

e) Have him describe how they form their church vision.

f) Have him fully describe his typical church planning meeting.

g) Ask him if he takes specific steps to keep church planning prayer-filled and God-focused.

WHAT QUESTIONS WOULD YOU ADD???

h) _____

_____

i) _____

_____

j) _____

_____

k) _____

_____

Financial Questions

a) Figure his churches' financial giving patterns in comparison with attendance patterns.

b) What are his own personal patterns of giving?

c) How does he calculate a tithe?

d) What does he teach and preach about giving beyond the local church?

e) Have him describe his typical church stewardship campaigns in detail.

f) Ask his beliefs about funding building (or other) church projects. What does he believe about church debt?

g) What percentages did his churches give to denominational or associational ministries?

h) Is he deeply committed to the Cooperative Program as well as associational and state giving?

i) Ask him to describe his involvement with Women's Mission Ministries.

j) Have missions giving and projects grown significantly under his leadership?

WHAT QUESTIONS WOULD YOU ADD???

k) _____

_____

l) _____

_____

m)_____

_____

n) _____

_____

Spiritual Disciplines Questions

a) Ask him to fully describe what he does and its average length.

b) Get him to describe his study habits and his strategies for continuing personal growth.

c) Is a strong daily prayer time an absolute priority to this candidate?

d) Ask whether he ever takes personal retreats for an extended two or three days in prayer and spiritual cleansing.

e) Have him describe any special promises that he has received from God.

f) Ask whether fasting is a part of his life.

g) Does he himself commit to a regular time in the prayer room?

h) Ask him to describe the prayer ministries and meetings he would lead a church to develop.

i) Research church baptism ratios in each of his previous pastorates.

j) Research the prospect's church attendance growth in direct comparison with population trends in the surrounding community or region.

k) Have the candidate thoroughly describe his biblical philosophy of pastoral ministry and leadership.

l) Ask for specific ways his ministry philosophy has been implemented in his former churches.

m) What leadership materials and conference has he attended?

n) Is there a particular book that largely describes his leadership style?

o) Ask the candidate his views of the changing philosophies of how to build healthy churches in today's world.

p) Have him describe in detail his views of the "seeker-friendly" church.

q) Ask which of the modern books on innovative church growth he has read. Which ones does he like?

WHAT QUESTIONS WOULD YOU ADD???

r) _____

_____

s) _____

_____

t) _____

_____

u) _____

_____

Preaching Questions

    a) Have the prospect thoroughly describe his preaching philosophy and his patterns.

    b) Does he do mostly expository preaching through books of the Bible or mostly topics and series?

    c) Does he consistently preach the whole "council of God" or stay with a few popular themes and subjects?

    d) Ask the candidate if he is proficient in Greek and Hebrew as an aid to his Bible study.

    e) Ask him to give you the names of several commentaries he uses.

    f) Determine in detail what type of prayer meetings and prayer ministries his churches have developed.

    g) Did he start them and did he have a strong active role in leading them?

WHAT QUESTIONS WOULD YOU ADD???

    h) _____

_____

    i) _____

_____

j) _____

   _____

k) _____

   _____

Sunday School/Small Group Questions

a) What does he believe about trying to minister and relate to all age groups?

b) Ask him to describe the specific strategies he uses to maintain closeness and trust with each age group.

c) What kind of Sunday School growth and evangelism strategies has he employed?

d) How does he secure good church involvement?

e) Ask the prospect's view and practices concerning cell groups and home Bible studies. If he has used this strategy, ask him to describe how it was administrated and rate its effectiveness. What were its strengths and weaknesses? Determine the type of materials and leadership structure he has employed. Does he see this approach as a primary ongoing strategy or a periodic emphases?

WHAT QUESTIONS WOULD YOU ADD???

f) _____

   _____

g) _____

_____

h) _____

_____

i) _____

_____

Church Discipline Questions

What does he believe about church discipline?

a) Have him specifically describe his beliefs and give any examples of times he has executed discipline concerning staff, lay leaders or church members.

b) What does he see as issues that would warrant church disciplinary action?

c) How would he define the blessings and dangers of church discipline?

WHAT QUESTIONS WOULD YOU ADD???

d) _____

_____

e) _____

_____

f) _____

_____

g) _____

_____

Spiritual Gifts Questions

a) What are his specific views concerning gifts of healing and speaking in tongues?

b) What are his typical patterns in regards to the corporate practice of the spiritual gifts?

c) Does his beliefs and patterns match yours?

d) Has he faced such battles in the past and if so, how did he handle them?

e) Describe a few hypothetical cases in which spiritual gifts could become a controversy and specifically ask how he would address the various issues.

WHAT QUESTIONS WOULD YOU ADD???

f) _____

_____

g) _____

_____

h) _____

_____

i) _____

_____

Worship/Music Questions ✓

a) Has he encountered "worship wars" and if so, how did he handle it?

b) What is his philosophy of leading a church through changing worship styles?

c) Have him describe in detail the music and worship styles he would most encourage.

d) Is he committed to Sunday and Wednesday evening services?

e) What is his opinion of moving Sunday night worship to home cell groups?

l) Have the prospect give several specific examples of finding God's direction for setting and reaching specific church goals or projects

m) Determine if he has a multi-level strategy of developing a "regional" church.

WHAT QUESTIONS WOULD YOU ADD???

n) _____

_____

o) _____

_____

p) _____

_____

q) _____

_____

Leadership Style Questions

a) What is his leadership style in terms of personality, organizational and biblical principles of leadership?

b) Does he lead more by pastoral decree, consensus building with lay leadership or something in the middle?

c) How often does he convene the church council and how are they used?

d) Ask him to fully describe his beliefs and practices concerning pastoral authority.

e) Have him describe his specific strategies for giving strong leadership to key committees while still giving freedom for lay leadership to do their job.

f) What specific strategies has he employed to develop and encourage lay leadership?

g) What is his pattern and beliefs concerning office hours?

h) Ask the candidate to describe his experience and strategies for leading a multi-staff team to good cohesion and teamwork.

i) How does he establish accountability and oversight in his staff?

WHAT QUESTIONS WOULD YOU ADD???

j) _____

_____

k) _____

_____

l) _____

_____

m) _____

_____

Business Meeting/Accountability Questions

Have him describe (in detail) his beliefs about church business meetings.

a) How often does he conduct them?

b) Who moderates them?

c) How much detail does he recommend in the regular financial reports?

d) What kind of accountability is he accustomed to in previous churches?

e) Is he willing to submit to a yearly meeting with personnel or pastoral committee (if appropriate?)

f) What kind of financial oversight does he recommend in a church?

g) Does he recommend yearly outside audits, etc.?

h) What are the type things he thinks the church should vote upon at business meetings?

WHAT QUESTIONS WOULD YOU ADD???

i) _____

_____

j) _____

_____

k) _____

_____

l) _____

_____

Deacon/Elder Ministry Questions

a) Ask him to describe his beliefs and practices regarding deacon/elder ministry and leadership in detail.

b) How does he work to maintain a close cooperative relationship with his deacons/elders?

c) What is his belief and practice on ordaining or utilizing deacons/elders who are divorced and/or remarried?

d) Ask him to fully describe his view of using (or not using) church deacons/elders.

e) How does he see the differing roles of deacons and elders?

f) Would he lead his church toward an elder led church?

WHAT QUESTIONS WOULD YOU ADD???

g) _____

_____

h) _____

_____

i) _____

_____

j) _____

_____

Theological/Denominational Questions

a) Ask him if he believes there is any "mixture of error" in the Bible.

b) Does he believe the Genesis account of creation is literal or figurative?

c) Ask if he believes all the biblical miracles were real events.

d) Ask him to describe his view of different translations of the Bible.

e) What translation does he typically use in preaching or teaching?

f) How does he classify his biblical, theological and denominational allegiance?

g) Is he a conservative, fundamentalist, moderate, etc?

h) Is he a five point Calvinist/Armenian?

i) Have him explain his answers very thoroughly.

WHAT QUESTIONS WOULD YOU ADD???

a) _____

_____

b) _____

_____

c) _____

_____

d) _____

_____

Denominational Leadership

e) Is he involved in several committees and has he held high elected positions in the association, state, or national convention?

f) If so, what steps did he take to keep it from interfering with his pastorate?

g) Does he see himself in increasing roles of local, state or national denominational leadership?

h) Has he been heavily involved in local, state or national politics? (Either government or denominational) *It speaks very well when the denomination sees your pastor as a leader. In fact, great pastors usually do exert considerable leadership beyond their church. In general, you want to make sure it is not a passion to the point of interfering with his pastoral role!

i) Also ask how much he wants the church involved in state and associational activities.

j) Does he have outside ministries to the point they would seriously divide his focus and passion? A healthy balance is the desire. (In general, you want neither an isolationist nor a pastor over-involved in outside causes.)

WHAT QUESTIONS WOULD YOU ADD???

k) _____

_____

l) _____

_____

m) _____

_____

n) _____

_____

Miscellaneous "Extremism" Questions

Determine if he has any views that might be considered extreme or could easily become controversial.

a) In other words, does he have any views or patterns that are atypical of your church, group or denomination?

b) If applicable or a concern, ask questions about music or worship styles, any practice or views of spiritual gifts that are atypical for your church or denomination, the use of elders, cell groups, alien immersion, requirements for receiving members into the church (baptism, statement, etc.), Bible translation controversies, the use of women as deacons or teachers, extreme emphasis on the doctrine of election, personal wedding policies and beliefs, views on homosexuality as it relates to morality, church membership or church involvement, committee selection process, deacon election procedures and qualifications, business meeting frequency and style of leading them, frequency and style of leading Lord Suppers, his views on tithing, Masonic lodge, isolation from associational involvement, etc.

c) Inform the candidate of any of these areas that your church has or is currently dealing with as a body. Neither candidate nor church need any 'surprises' in these areas.

WHAT QUESTIONS WOULD YOU ADD???

d) _____

_____

e) _____

_____

f) _____

_____

g) _____

_____

Integrity Questions

a) Ask the candidate's specific strategies for protecting his reputation and guarding his morality.

b) What are his policies of counseling or visiting women by himself?

c) What are his strategies to prevent any exposure to internet pornography (or any appearance of evil?)

d) Does he have accountability prayer partners that have the right to evaluate and speak into his life?

e) How often does he meet with accountability partners?

WHAT QUESTIONS WOULD YOU ADD???

f) _____

_____

g) _____

_____

h) _____

_____

i) _____

_____

"Therefore, since we are surrounded by such a great cloud of witnesses, let us throw off everything that hinders and the sin that so easily entangles, and let us run with perseverance the race marked out for us."
Hebrews 12:1

Appendix E- <u>Sample Interview Questions for Pastor & Wife</u>

1. Share with us about your childhood and family background.
   a. What are some of your best memories in growing up?
   b. How do you think God used your background to help prepare you to be a minister's wife?
   c. Tell us about your hobbies and interests.

2. Share your salvation testimony& what you love about ministry.
   a. What are your primary spiritual gifts?
   b. How does God most often use your spiritual gifts?
   c. What ministries do you enjoy the most and least?

3. How did you meet your husband?
   a. Tell us a little about your wedding and early years of marriage.
   b. Was your husband a minister when you married him?
   c. How do you see your role as a pastor's wife?
   d. What do you see as the most important elements of being a pastor's wife?

4. In one sentence, what does it mean to be a good pastor's wife?

a. What brings you the most joy and fulfillment in being a pastor's wife?

b. What are some of the greatest challenges?

c. How could our church minimize these challenges and support you and your family?

5. How do you and your husband guard the strength of your marriage?

a. Describe your patterns of family devotions. (In term of frequency and what you do.)

b. How often do you take time to get away together?

6. Has there been a time in the church when someone badly hurt you?

a. Please tell us about that situation.

7. Describe some of your most challenging ministry experiences.

a. As husband and wife, how did you get through those times and what did you learn?

b. What have been your greatest personal challenges and how did you get through these trials?

c. What did you learn from your times of struggle?

8. What are your primary feelings about a potential move?

a. Why do you think it might be God's will for your husband to move to another church?

b. How do you think your children would handle a move?

c. How would you want us to specifically pray for each child in particular?

WHAT QUESTIONS WOULD YOU ADD?

9. _____

_____

10. _____

_____

11. _____

_____

12. _____

_____

13. _____

_____

14. _____

_____

15. _____

_____

"Now may the God of peace, who through the blood of the eternal covenant brought back from the dead our Lord Jesus, that great Shepherd of the sheep,[21] equip you with everything good for doing his will, and may he work in uswhat is pleasing to him, through Jesus Christ, to whom be glory for ever and ever. Amen." **Hebrews 13:20-21**

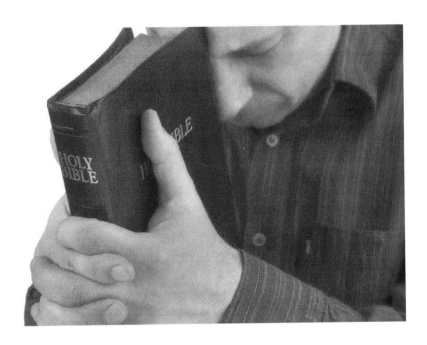

Appendix F- Pastor Search Process Chart

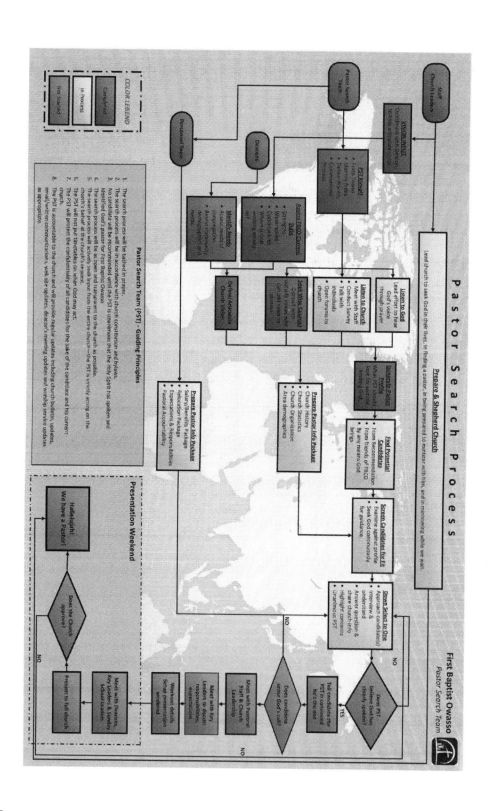

Appendix G- Resources

Book Resources

Seeking God to Seek A Pastor by Dr. Greg Frizzell

Side-Stepping Landmines: Five Principles for Pastor Search Teams by Joel Rainey

Pastor Search Committee Handbook by Robert Sheffield

Web Resources

http://web.kybaptist.org/web/doc/PastorSearchwb.pdf

http://thomrainer.com/2014/07/21/five-pleas-pastors-pastor-search-committees/

http://www.ubahouston.org/filerequest/4616

Made in the USA
Middletown, DE
18 August 2017